Upcycled Chic
and Modern Hacks

Upcycled Chic

and Modern Hacks

Thrifty Ways for Stylish Homes

**Liz Bauwens and
Alexandra Campbell**

Photography by Simon Brown

CICO BOOKS
LONDON NEW YORK

TO: Lois, Finn, and Milo Brown and Freddie and Rosie Iron

Published in 2015 by CICO Books
An imprint of Ryland Peters & Small Ltd
20–21 Jockey's Fields   341 E 116th St
London WC1R 4BW   New York, NY 10029

www.rylandpeters.com

10 9 8 7 6 5 4 3 2 1

Text, design, and photography © CICO
Books 2015

A CIP catalog record for this book is
available from the Library of Congress
and the British Library.

ISBN: 978 1 78249 185 9

Printed in China

Editor: Helen Ridge
Designer: Louise Leffler
Photographer: Simon Brown

Managing editor: Gillian Haslam
In-house designer: Fahema Khanam
Art director: Sally Powell
Production director: Patricia Harrington
Publishing manager: Penny Craig
Publisher: Cindy Richards

For digital editions, visit
www.cicobooks.com/apps.php

Previous page: An old school cupboard door, still with sums etched
into the wood, makes a kitchen cupboard for upcycler Mark Rochester,
along with a 1930s factory clock and a contemporary fridge.

Above: An old drum—too battered for making music—upcycled as
a table by Clio The Muse for the Goldfinger Factory. She stripped back
the layers, then built up the decoration with vintage paper and gold paint,
adding a glass top.

Opposite: A pine table upcycled by Clio The Muse for the Goldfinger
Factory. She scrubbed it down to remove the orangey pine effect, added
a wash of white and painted the knife, fork, and spoon design on. It can
be cleaned with a simple wipe.

contents

introduction

Upcycling and hacking are two new and important words in today's decorating dictionary.

Upcycling is giving an item a new lease of life by using it in a different context or turning it into something else. Redundant pieces of industrial furniture, from dentists' cabinets to office chairs, can take on a new role in the home, while discarded CDs or blancmange molds can be made into lampshades, and old floorboards into kitchen units. Meanwhile, in the upcycled garden, drainpipes or old boots become original planters.

Hacking is transforming an ordinary piece into something special. This could be done by making the legs longer on a basic chain-store kitchen, bedroom, or bathroom unit, or changing the top, the handles, or the doors. You could paint it, strip it, glaze it, or cover it in fabric, even giftwrap.

By upcycling and hacking, it's possible to create a designer look at a value-for-money price. But it's not just a question of saving money—it's about making your home look different and giving it personality. It also concerns craftsmanship, reusing materials that would otherwise have been discarded or discovering techniques that would otherwise be lost. Before industrialization, nothing was wasted—everything was used and reused.

With upcycling and hacking, there'll always be a story to tell—whether about buying and bringing a piece home or about the person who gave it to you—and those stories and memories are particular to you. Maybe you were given a hand-me-down by a friend or relative, or you spotted an old door or a 1950s filing cabinet in a junk shop on a day out. You repair it or you put it in a contemporary room where the patina of age creates atmosphere. Or you buy a cheap lamp, paint it, and change the shade. And everyone asks you where it came from.

So what do you need to know to upcycle or hack? If you love rummaging, that's the perfect starting point. Search, and keep searching. Look in chain stores and junk shops for

Left: This bedside table is made from a dish-rack, topped with a pewter tray. Actress Joanne McQuinn found the lamp and shade in a junk shop. The fabric of the shade was ripped so she re-covered it herself, using a silk scarf.

Above: This child's armchair in Joanne's daughter's room came from an estate sale shop.

inexpensive items. Then browse in smart stores, and flick through magazines or books, such as this one, for inspiration. They are an ideal starting point, and here we've also included practical advice wherever necessary.

Hacking requires care and attention, rather than expertise. Most paints, for example, are supplied with good instructions on how to use them. But when it comes to plumbing or electrics, consult a professional—inexpert plumbing and electrical work are the commonest causes of house fires and floods!

Upcycling and hacking undoubtedly save money, but don't overlook the extra costs you may incur. You may have to pay for professional repairs or alterations. Although it can still be cheaper to get a carpenter to adapt a chain-store unit than it is to commission a new one, you shouldn't expect to pay next to nothing for the work. And re-covering a chair or sofa will entail the cost of the fabric, plus the professional upholstery expertise, which could run into many hours' worth of time. And for those large items that you can't get home yourself, such as sofas, chests, or dining tables, there are transport costs that need to be factored in.

Above all, upcycling and hacking should be fun. Instead of trawling a characterless shopping mall, filled with all the same international chains, explore a historic town or market instead. And if you happen to be walking down the smartest streets of New York, London, or Paris, browse the store windows—then see how you can adapt their ideas using cheaper furniture. Look through these pages for ideas and inspiration from the talented upcyclers and hackers who have generously allowed us to photograph their homes. We hope you enjoy the book.

Above left: Many people assume that once a clock is broken, then there's nothing to be done, but, like this 1930s factory clock, many can be repaired or a new quartz mechanism can be installed.
Above: One of artist Lucy Dickens' collection of vintage toys, used as a door stop.
Right: French bistro chairs in Lucy Dickens' house. Ex-café and restaurant chairs have now become popular in the home, and are easy to search for on the internet or via specialist second-hand sites.

chapter one
kitchens

The kitchen is probably the room where you will spend the most time—and the most money. But you don't have to choose between making a huge investment in a designer kitchen and settling for an ordinary, mass-market look. You can add personality by upcycling secondhand furniture, china, and accessories. And you can hack chain-store kitchen units to make them look the way you want. You could go crisp and modern—or vintage and colorful. Take a look at these pages and let your imagination fly.

color *and paint hacks*

This kitchen belongs to artist Thomasina Smith. It's contemporary and individual, with a twentieth-century modern look about it. However, the units are standard chain-store purchases made of inexpensive laminate, which have simply been sanded down and painted.

Paint is great for hacking, but don't just think about which color to use. All the various brands of paint have different chemical bases, which reflect light differently. You will also tend to find a higher intensity of pigment in the more expensive paints. Here, Thomasina has used an environmentally friendly heritage paint, which has a 40 percent higher intensity of pigment. This means that the colors are distinct, but not bright or harsh. Don't be tempted to save money by trying to match paint colors across brands—find the paint with the color, texture, and effect you want. The actual cost of paint for a few units will be a minor factor in the total budget for kitting out a kitchen.

Above left: Thomasina describes these cabinet colors as an "Indian-Caribbean palette." The kitchen looks as if it dates back to the birth of the modern kitchen—the house itself was built in the 1920s. She felt it was important for the kitchen to remain true to its twentieth-century heritage, rather than giving it a Victorian or a contemporary look.

Above: A pull-out refrigerator drawer is a great idea (although Thomasina says it's a bit tricky to clean). She gave the mass-market units attractive handles—always a good hack.

Opposite: Note how Thomasina has painted the upper wall units white, so they "fade" into the walls. The floor is elm, not recycled but "second-grade" elm, so cheaper than regular flooring elm and with more character.

What we call "modern design" has its roots in the early and mid-twentieth century. After the Great War of 1914–18 turned society upside down, fewer servants were employed to do housework. Domestic design responded to the change by becoming more attractive and easier to use or clean.

"Mid-century modern" is the term used to describe furniture designed between 1950 and the early 1970s. Such pieces have simple, clean lines and are ideal for kitchens. They are often made of easy-wear materials such as plastics, wood composites, and resin, which were originally developed for military use in World War II.

Mid-century modern fell out of favor in the 1970s recession, when the design world was engulfed in a tsunami of nostalgic florals, chintz, and Victorian pine. But in the last decade, people have been rediscovering and upcycling mid-century modern for its combination of style and practicality. As kitchens morphed into kitchen-living rooms, mid-century modern chairs and sofas offered comfort and good looks, as well as being easier to clean than chintz and velvet.

Opposite: Thomasina took down walls in the kitchen to open up the space into a kitchen-living room. Scandinavian furniture leads the mid-century modern trend, and this mustard-yellow sofa is a 1970s Danish design. Although you would have to pay a premium for original designs by the likes of Eero Saarinen and Arne Jacobsen, it's worth looking out for pieces by less well-known names. The curtain is made of that most mid-century modern of fabrics—burlap (hessian). Both it and the lamp came from chain stores.

Above right: A leftover square of translucent fabric is pinned to the window for privacy. The syrup can is purely for decoration—upcycling means seeing the beauty in everyday objects and turning them into pieces of art.

Right: The flowers are arranged in glass pitchers and recycled jars. The tall measuring glasses were acquired from a science laboratory at a college that was closing down.

Many shops, auction houses, and online sites now specialize in mid-century modern, while some of the original furniture companies from that time, such as Parker Knoll, are still in business, making the same designs.

One of the most important points about Scandinavian mid-century modern is that it brought beautiful, practical furniture to the masses, which meant that a great deal of it was produced. Look online or in junk shops for simple shapes, slim legs, and strong, distinctive colors. The chairs and tables were well made but many designs would be difficult to repair, so don't buy anything that's unsteady. Fabric, however, is easily replaced.

When friends or relatives are having a clear-out, keep an eye open for classic modern style. Sometimes upcycling is just a question of context: put your grandmother's chair in your contemporary interior and its clean lines will sing out.

Hand-me-downs and exchanges are at the heart of upcycling. Don't just throw something out but see if someone else would like it. Thomasina often exchanges her paintings for those of fellow artists, such as the picture on page 14. But more mundane items, like refrigerators, dishwashers, and washing machines, are often found through local exchange schemes, such as Freecycle.

Above left: The pink cushion is a recent purchase from a department store. Thomasina's mother bought the portrait at auction in the 1970s, and its frame at a separate auction. "It's my favorite possession," says Thomasina. *Left:* Thomasina upcycled three regular milk bottles with paint and made them into decorative objects. She was inspired by the work of Giorgio Morandi, an Italian artist who painted pictures of domestic objects in soft, chalky shades in the 1950s. You could also paint glass jars or vases. *Opposite:* The chair is a classic Windsor chair design. First appearing in the seventeenth century, the design became increasingly elaborate until the twentieth century, when several furniture brands started to produce simpler, modern versions. You can find recent Windsor chairs in almost any auction house or junk shop, but check that the legs and back are well jointed together. The vase came from a ceramicist with whom Thomasina shared a studio. "He used to throw away pots he wasn't satisfied with, so I asked for this one," she says.

The basics in this kitchen—the units, shelves, and tiles—are low-cost chain-store purchases, but they have been transformed with a lick of paint and by adding special touches. Mixing cheap with expensive, or mainstream with unusual, is a core hacking trick.

kitchen *hacks*

Although there is a vintage feel to this kitchen, the units and tiles all come from standard chain-store outlets. The house belongs to Posy Gentles, who specializes in garden renovation. When she bought it, the kitchen units and worktop were made of beech, there were brushed stainless-steel handles on the cupboard doors, and wall units loomed over the worktop.

The kitchen is long and narrow, and Posy felt that the wall units made the room seem even narrower. So she removed them, putting in their place two sets of open shelves. The absence of doors gives the room a much more spacious feel. Then she painted the whole kitchen—units and walls—in the same vintage shade of white. Having them the same color also helps to make the room appear more open and light.

Above, left to right: Posy has picked up most of her china in yard sales and thrift shops. The cream tiles were the cheapest she could find, but she also bought a few colored tiles, which should have been a lot more expensive but were going cheap because they were remnants. Posy and her partner, Rutledge Turnlund, cut the tiles into different shapes and tiled the wall in an abstract pattern. The vintage cooking timer was bought on eBay.

Opposite: The beech units were painted white and given new, white china handles—inexpensive purchases from a hardware store. The worktop was also beech, but Posy sanded it down, stained and oiled it, so that it now resembles teak. The bowls and glassware are a mix of junk finds and chain-store buys. The open shelves were made by a friend, with the paneled back painted a chalky heritage green.

The dining area at the far end of Posy's long, thin kitchen has French doors, which originally opened into the room, taking up valuable space. However, turning them around, so that they now open outward onto the garden, has created more living space inside.

The awkward position of the garden door, so close to the perpendicular wall, made hanging a curtain difficult. Rutledge solved the problem by fixing one end of regular thick dowling, bought at a hardware store, to the wall, and adding a finial that he found in a junk shop to the other end. Painting it all concealed the join—a practical and money-saving solution. The curtain hooks are a mix of styles. Most of them came from Posy's grandmother's house, while the curtains themselves are from a previous home.

Posy collected the dining chairs one by one or in pairs from junk shops over a period of time. In a mix of styles from the 1950s and '60s, all are pink with tubular legs, making a distinctive co-ordinating collection around the table. Made of Formica and different plastics, they're hardwearing as well as good-looking.

Opposite: Posy sold her previous rectangular table on eBay and, with the proceeds, bought this round one, which fits the space better, from a secondhand store. The stoneware jars on the dresser were found on a dumpsite by her daughter.

Above left and overleaf right: Posy painted the display cabinet, lined it with wrapping paper, and changed the handle to a round porcelain one. Two Waterford crystal glasses were found in a rummage sale; the 1950s gold-rimmed ones at thrift stores. The crab painting is by Norfolk artist Paul Bommer.

Above right: The cups are the mid-twentieth century Twin Tone range from Poole Pottery, which Posy collects from internet auctions and rummage sales.

Overleaf left: The "No Cakes" cabinet was upcycled by Nick Kenny, who creates kitchens and bathrooms from recycled and found materials. The map picture is a piece of wrapping paper, and the vases are San Pellegrino bottles.

There is a growing interest in upcycling salvaged retail or industrial furniture and fittings, and repurposing them for domestic use. The cabinet shown opposite is a good example. Originally, a dentist's cabinet, it belongs to garden designer Fern Alder and suits her kitchen perfectly, offering lots of convenient storage and a distinctive style. Generally, twentieth-century industrial design, materials, and workmanship are of a high quality and adapt well to domestic use, offering something that is tough, hardwearing, and full of character.

Look out for chairs and cabinets from doctors' and dentists' surgeries, opticians, hairdressers, and barbers. Storage units from old drugstores are particularly beautiful, although they have become quite pricey. Old store fixtures can also offer wonderful storage and style, as can furniture, fittings, and lighting from factories and schools.

The internet is the starting place for hunting down industrial and retail salvage. Use search terms such as "vintage industrial," "vintage apothecary," and "vintage store fixtures" (or "vintage shop fittings"). There are architectural salvage stores and flea markets all over the USA, UK, and Europe, and you may also find the occasional piece in a junk shop.

Opposite: The mid-twentieth-century dentist's cabinet makes perfect storage in Fern's kitchen: compact and easily accessible. Attractive storage jars are displayed behind glass doors, while the more unsightly kitchen paraphernalia remains hidden. The easy-to-clean marble top adds to the cabinet's usefulness.

Above right: Posy found the electric factory clock in a dumpster (skip). Although it wasn't working, it was easily repaired with a new electric mechanism and now keeps good time. The little picture below it is a 1910 postcard, which Posy found when she was a child. The kitchen chalkboard was originally used to keep scores in darts matches, while the weighing scales came from a delicatessen—a gift from the owner.

Right: You can still find lots of mid-century modern storage jars in thrift shops or secondhand stores—these are from the 1960s—as well as on the internet. But there are also some very stylish vintage designs now being produced by chain stores at reasonable prices.

Upcycling is about creating personality in a home—and turning something ordinary into something special. It isn't always cheaper to buy from big companies. Sometimes it can be surprisingly thrifty to have a piece custom-made.

custom-made *but affordable*

The open shelves in Lucy Dickens's kitchen shown opposite have been handmade in Norfolk oak, which would normally attract a hefty price tag. But Lucy, an artist, costed it up and found that it was cheaper to have them made, rather than buying from a chain store, because she excluded the kind of work that is more intricate and takes longer to do—there are no drawers or cupboards. This approach would work particularly well in a small kitchen, as cupboard doors that open out take up a lot of valuable space. You don't have to use new wood either in this kind of kitchen—people have been known to recycle church pews or scaffolding boards.

The key to getting a custom-made kitchen at a bargain price tag is to use pieces of freestanding furniture in place of drawers and doors, such as a butcher's-block table, a stand-alone cupboard, or a chest of drawers, to provide additional storage.

Opposite: The open shelves are handmade but the simplicity of their design makes them very affordable. The central unit is a freestanding French butcher's-block table, with a zinc worktop and drawers for extra storage. The pendant lights are from a factory, while the flagstones are original to the house. A worn and weathered floor is very attractive, so don't automatically rip out or cover over old wood or stone.

Above left: Wine corks bound together with a metal band are used as heatproof mats.

Above center: Find old-fashioned weighing scales in thrift shops and yard sales.

Above right: Lucy keeps her decorative forks in an open wicker carrying basket—so convenient for setting the table.

Left: The three drawers in the butcher's-block table are the only ones in Lucy's kitchen. Upcycled baskets and crates offer alternative storage. Convenient, portable, and attractive, they house often-used items such as knives and forks, logs, and vegetables.

Above: This old stationery basket, once used in an office to marshal paperwork, now has a new life as a vegetable basket. Vintage office equipment works well in upcycling, but prices are rising as people begin to appreciate its design and production qualities. However, there are still bargains to be found on the internet and in specialist stores.

Opposite: White tiles, white walls, and a white butler's sink keep this look clean and simple. Everything is on show in this open-plan kitchen, so having similar key elements gives a sense of cohesion. Even though the various wood elements aren't the same, they are in similar tones.

Storage is a major issue in any kitchen, but often the solution is just a question of looking at things differently. Lucy's kitchen originally had an additional door leading from a corridor. As this wasn't strictly necessary, she had the back of the corridor blocked in to create a larder.

Rather than installing as many storage units as you can in your kitchen, start the other way around. Make a list of everything you use regularly and always need at hand, and another list of those things that you use only occasionally. Store the items accordingly. If you have a garage or a storeroom, putting up a set of shelves for rarely used china, for example, can free up a lot of valuable space.

contemporary *hacks*

The kitchen that came with writer Penny Rich's new-build apartment was completely standard. She had no choice in its style or decoration, and as she only had a small budget, she couldn't rip it out or even change all the doors. When she moved in, the upper cupboards were cream, as were the walls, which she found "dingy." In addition, the kitchen, which formed part of the living area, was carpeted—also in cream. Sometimes, changing just one element can make all the difference to an interior, and by swapping the cream for white, Penny made the space crisp, modern, and bright.

She changed the cream cupboard doors of the upper units to white, painted the walls white, and made one big financial investment: a white, poured resin floor. "I researched flooring, and this was neither cheap nor expensive. It's about average for new flooring. And it's very durable and easy to clean—it's used in gyms a lot. It's also perfect for a new-build because it needs a flat floor."

Opposite: White walls, black-and-white cupboard doors, and a black refrigerator make the standard kitchen in Penny's apartment look dramatic. The freestanding unit on casters is a recycled workbench from a school laboratory and provides an extra work surface. The white resin floor not only makes the room lighter but gives it an unusual, stylish edge.

Above: Penny's apartment is small, so she made the most of the available space by having this kitchen storage unit made to fit exactly between the upper and lower units. She measured everything that she wanted to keep there exactly, so not an inch of space is wasted.

upcycle *by collecting*

This kitchen belongs to artist and sculptor Tim Braden. He has collected the chairs, china, and pendant lamps one by one over a period of time. He always keeps an eye out for pieces to add to his collections, and has even brought things home when they've been left on the street—the big table, battered and spattered with paint, is one of his larger "street finds."

The basics in Tim's kitchen are regular standard units that have been made to look special with chalk paints. Although chalky, textured paints aren't usually recommended for kitchens simply because they're harder to clean. But if you like the effect, then go for it. You will just have to repaint a little more often.

The key to creating a successful collection is to turn yourself into a mini-expert on, for example, a certain style of chair, china, or furniture. It's harder these days to find a bargain now that pieces can be easily researched on the internet, but if, say, the chairs you have chosen to collect look very ordinary, other people may not bother with them. And if you are primed to spot a certain shape or pattern amid a pile of junk, you'll recognize it more quickly than anyone else.

Above left: This spotted tea service is from Georgia, when it was one of the Soviet republics. Tim found the pieces one by one, which explains why they are all slightly different versions of the same pattern.

Left: While driving through Hampshire in the south of England, Tim spotted this sign offering fish for sale on a roadside stall. The stall-holder was initially reluctant to part with it—"How am I going to sell my fish?"—but Tim got his way in the end. He put it in an exhibition and titled it "English Landscape Painting." Now it lives in his kitchen. It shows that it's worth persevering if you like something enough!

Opposite: These chairs, by mid-century modern Dutch designer Friso Kramer, were produced so widely that Tim even found a couple of them on the street. The others he bought, one by one, and some of them he painted. These days, Friso Kramer chairs are mostly found on eBay and in specialist stores, but you may be lucky enough to spot one in a junk shop. The table was also a street find—Tim sanded down the top and painted the legs a chalky gray.

As an artist, it's natural for Tim to upcycle furniture by painting it, but anyone can do it. As well as painting the chairs and the table, his kitchen is given a sense of unity by painting the seating—an old plan chest, which is also used for storage—in a similar dark blue shade to the kitchen units.

Painting furniture isn't just a question of choosing the right color. It's important to prepare the surfaces by cleaning and sanding them thoroughly. If the furniture has been waxed, clean the wax off first with wire wool. Then use a primer, which will make the paint adhere better. Once this is dry, apply two thin coats of paint, allowing each one to dry completely before sanding down lightly between each coat. If you haven't painted furniture before, practice first on something small and inexpensive, such as a little chest from a junk shop.

Opposite: An old map chest from a school classroom is now used as seating. Tim painted it and his mother made the cushions.

Above left: School science laboratories in the 1950s were equipped with wonderful teak surfaces. Tim upcycled his kitchen worktop from a science workbench, filling in the holes every few feet where a Bunsen burner was originally fitted. The clock came from a flea market in Marrakesh, while the red-and-white metal tiles were once used to mark out "No Entry" areas.

Above: Vintage milk bottles (these ones came from Scarlet & Violet) in lovely solid shapes and colors can be used as decoration or repurposed as vases or water pitchers for the table.

industrial *upcycling*

This kitchen belongs to Mark Rochester, whose company, Rochesters, upcycles industrial and other salvaged materials to turn into furniture for the home. He lives here with his artist wife, Talya Baldwin, and their children. "Everything in my house is upcycled," he says. This has meant that he has had to make window and door openings larger in order to fit salvaged window frames and doors.

Apart from the present-day tiles, stove, and refrigerator, everything in this kitchen has come from a nineteenth- or twentieth-century factory, farm, store, or café. The large stone sink with its swirly sides, however, was found almost buried in a nearby wood. "It took quite a lot of digging out, and I had to get help to carry it," recalls Mark. The pendant lights and the clock came from a factory that had closed down.

Above: Industrial salvage often needs work before it's ready for a new role in the home. For example, the pretty "table" above is the bottom half of an agricultural chaff-cutter, once used on a farm at harvest time. Mark removed the top half of the machinery and added the tabletop. Behind it is a set of shelves that started life in a Victorian clothing store. The refrigerator is a present-day copy of a 1950s model.

Opposite: The plate rack came from a dairy, where it was used to dry off milk bottles that had been disinfected, ready for refilling. The faucets (taps) below, with the chrome worn off to reveal the brass, were originally in a garden.

When factories closed down, amalgamated, or were modernized, machinery and fittings were often thrown away or lost. Now there's a growing recognition of the solid materials and workmanship that were used to make them: "If something can survive 80 years in a factory, it can withstand family life," says Mark Rochester. "And some things, such as light switches, are made of better materials than those we use now."

Clockwise, from top left: A bib faucet (tap) is usually used outside but also looks good in the kitchen; the corner of a stone sink discovered in a wood; GECoRay shop window lighting from the 1920s; 1920s factory light switches can easily be wired up to work in modern homes; plates from the staff canteen of the Dean, Smith & Grace foundry in West Yorkshire; a vintage Coughtrie bulkhead light from a factory; a champagne riddling rack once used in a winery; a 1950s vegetable rack from the days before refrigerators were commonplace; screw-top storage jars; a 1950s factory switch; the edge of a discarded stone sink; silverware is kept in an obsolete, industrial bread-making mold.

Mark and Talya's home is a nineteenth-century mill-worker's cottage but restoration work in the 1980s had apparently stripped out all the character. However, the couple were delighted to discover original Yorkshire stone flagstones in the kitchen once they removed the twentieth-century asphalt floor.

Replacing nondescript doors and window frames with salvaged pieces has also helped to inject some character back into the cottage. One door was found in the street; others were bought from junk yards. The door in the kitchen is from an old school and has childrens' sums scribbled into the wood. "I even use salvaged door hinges," says Mark.

The room is heated with a beautiful old radiator from a Victorian Methodist chapel. "An antique radiator takes longer to heat up, but it holds the warmth for longer, too," explains Mark. He advises taking care when buying one, however: "Cast-iron radiators are very heavy, which makes them difficult to transport safely. If they're not removed and installed carefully, then it's easy to break the internal seals, which will be very expensive to restore. If you buy from a reputable junk yard, they should have pressure-tested them. Always ask."

Opposite: The chest of drawers, with the original half-moon brass handles, came from a joinery workshop, although Mark had to put a top on it. The white-painted radiator alongside once heated a Victorian chapel.

Above: On the mezzanine level, the metal stand holding pots and pans, and a perforated metal box with kitchen utensils inside, is a 1940s engineer's stand from a foundry: "It's a sturdy factory build, and would once have held engineering equipment," says Mark. On the top shelf sits an old industrial bread mold—you can see the shape that the loaves would have been—which now holds silverware. The compartments are the perfect fit for knives, forks, and spoons.

Above: The family eats at an old French metal garden table, while sitting on factory chairs. Chairs like this, whether used in factories or schools, were made in their millions, so there are lots around on the vintage market. Some need work but many people like the weathered and battered look.

upcycle and hack

This unusual kitchen belongs to actress Joanne McQuinn, who has used both upcycling and hacking in its creation. She ordered the most basic MDF (medium-density fiberboard) carcasses from the internet for her kitchen units, and then asked a friend, Gerry Peachey, to make the doors.

Gerry makes shepherds' huts and dovecotes. He also collects old corrugated iron and pieces of painted wood—often floorboards—which he leaves in their battered range of colors and finishes, then repurposes. He has upcycled old, painted wood boards in a variety of shades of blue, green, gray, and black to make the doors for Joanne's kitchen cabinets. "He said that I would have to take what boards were available, so I didn't have any options in terms of color, but when the doors arrived they went perfectly with my blue and green tiles. I was over the moon," says Joanne.

Gerry also made the worksurface of sheet copper, which is laid over an ordinary MDF surface: "Sheet copper isn't as expensive as you might think," says Jo. "It was cheaper than a lot of worksurface materials and is naturally antibacterial, so it's ideal in a kitchen."

Above left: A closeup of the recycled painted boards used to make the kitchen cabinet doors. The metal handles came from a DIY store.
Left: Joanne has a few interesting pieces of vintage kitchenware, including this old-fashioned egg rack.
Opposite: The two open shelves, holding storage jars and vintage weighing scales, are made from old pieces of wood. "I use offcuts of other projects to make shelves," says Jo. "I never buy anything from 'proper shops'—I'm always looking for a cheaper option." The beautiful blue and green wall tiles are zelig tiles from Emery et Cie, the Brussels-based company that also supplied the patchwork floor tiles featured on pages 116–17. The enameled tiles are made from earth, using traditional techniques, in the city of Fez in Morocco. They are always plain, not patterned, and come in over 40 colors.

Above: Joanne reuses these very handsome French lemonade bottles by filling them with water for the dining table. They are reflected in the gleaming, sheet copper worksurface in the foreground. Although the copper marks easily, it creates an attractive, ever-changing patina. Being naturally antibacterial, it is very hygienic and so perfect for a kitchen.

Above right: The white butler's sink came from an architectural salvage store, while the breadbin is a 1950s vintage find. The 1950s saw an explosion of mass-market manufacturing, so it's not difficult to find genuine kitchenalia from that time at very cheap prices.

Many areas now run recycling wood projects. These are often community or charity organizations that have been set up to repurpose wood that would otherwise be thrown away. Their wood is usually cheaper than buying new and has the desirable worn patina you see on these pages.

Alternatively, look in junk yards or talk to friends and neighbors who are refurbishing their homes and may be thinking of throwing wood away. Check old boards for nails, splintered wood, or anything else that might cause injuries.

Old scaffolding boards, floorboards, wooden doors of all kinds (from cupboards, sheds, cabinets, or houses), old worktops, joists, beams, and decking offer opportunities for

reworking. Don't forget window frames, architectural moldings, and baseboards (skirting boards), which can be taken apart and reused to create unusual and characterful effects.

There may also be potential to reuse sheet material, such as plywood, chipboard, or old laminated flooring. Even old industrial pallets have valuable wood that can be reused. I've seen an ottoman made from a pallet. It was given short legs, which had been cut off a table, then padded with upholstery foam and covered with fabric. Scaffolding boards make strong shelving, while old doors can be transformed into kitchen tables. It's all perfect upcycling, and can give the most basic of mass-market kitchens an individual and unusual look.

Above: Joanne's farmhouse table with French bentwood café chairs. These were first invented in France by Thonet in the nineteenth century, which produced up to a million chairs a year. When the patent expired, others copied the design, so bentwood chairs filled cafés and restaurants all over the world. They've recently become popular in domestic kitchens, but there are still lots for sale. The pretty vegetable basket on the floor was bought in an estate sale shop (house clearance sale), while the steel pendant light is an ex-showroom display model—not a genuine vintage industrial light, but a bargain nevertheless.

junk yards and architectural salvage stores are a great hunting ground for upcyclers. Many also have a web presence, so you can rummage online for reclaimed building materials, garden and architectural antiques, and items rescued from demolition. If you're sharp-eyed, you can also pick up architectural salvage thrown out during a house renovation—but always seek permission from the owner first.

The blue-fronted cupboards you see on these pages originated as two pairs of shutters that Joanne bought at an architectural salvage store on spec, not knowing how she would use them or whether they would work or fit in her home. The purchase was inspired. Repurposed as the doors to two shelving units, the shutters, still in their original, weathered blue paint, have transformed the alcoves into something quite out of the ordinary.

One word of warning about architectural salvaged fittings, though. They are sometimes not as easy for architects and builders to work with as standard new items, and they may be reluctant to go along with your plans. However, reclaimed detail adds so much more character to a home, so do your best to make them see things your way.

Opposite: The two pairs of blue shutters were fitted to custom-made shelving units either side of the fireplace to create cupboards. Joanne painted the interiors in brown latex (emulsion) paint, then sealed them with clear varnish. She left the weathered patina of the shutter doors because the blue lends so much character to the room.

Above, from left to right: An old milk crate, upended, makes a perfect wine rack in Joanne's kitchen. Her collection of vintage china looks great against the brown-painted interior of the cupboards. The pretty table runner is, in fact, a 1950s cotton curtain. Don't feel constrained by what something was originally made for—use it however you like.

living rooms

The living room is where you stamp your personality on a home. Mixing up the contents—combining vintage and modern, upcycled and new—means that your living room will have individuality. Every piece in it has a story to tell. Today's trend is moving toward using industrial and office furniture in domestic interiors, along with salvaged fittings from schools, hospitals, banks, and retail outlets. Even buildings are being upcycled, with banks, churches, pubs, and community halls being turned into homes. This chapter is filled with ideas that you can adapt for your own house.

color *and light*

This is the living room of artist and sculptor Tim Braden. The house itself has been "upcycled," as it started life as a community center, with the living room originally a carport.

Tim's work uses color and light in interesting ways, and this is reflected in his home. Some of his paintings are almost monochrome, while others are brightly colored and vivid abstracts. The books in the custom-made bookcase have been put in order, although not by author or subject matter but according to the color of their spines. Tim's own painting of the bookcase is displayed appropriately on one of its shelves .

Artists make particularly good upcyclers because they tend to see shapes and colors without preconceptions—a child's toy or an old tin can, for example, can be just as beautiful to them as a vase or a piece of sculpture. They have also led the way in upcycling, out of necessity making "something from nothing" and using what others might consider waste and turning it into art. In the same way, when furnishing your own home, focus on shape and color rather than the original function of an object.

Left: This end of the living room is light and monochrome, in pale blue, gray, and white, which maximizes the natural light. Made of cast concrete, the ceiling is an original feature from the time the living room was the carport. It's been left unplastered, so that some of the building's original character survives. The furniture and decoration are a mix of modern and vintage: 1950s pendant lights, a contemporary Conran rug and sofa, and a Hockney print coexist happily with the antique map chest. Tim's mother-in-law made the abstract floral cushion.

Opposite: The architect's map chest doubles as a coffee table and storage—painting it white has increased the sense of light in the room. The bookcase was made to order, although Tim drew it out on the wall first, to ensure that everything would fit exactly.

The photographs on these two pages show an almost childlike use of primary colors—lovely bright blues, yellows, reds, and greens are mixed in a glorious jumble. An artist's eye understands color instinctively, but if you're not an artist and your aim is to mix old and new with vintage and modern, it really is worth learning about the color wheel.

You can find a color wheel online or in any serious book about color. The general principle is that there are three basic colors—red, yellow, and blue—and that all other colors are a blend of these three. Red, yellow, and blue are called "opposing colors." Then there is black and white, or how dark or light a color is. Dark green, for example, has more black in it than light green; very light green has more white. Often colors of a similar lightness and darkness (or tone) work well together, such as pale green and pale pink, or, as here, bright green, bright blue, and bright red. If you introduce a splash of an opposing color to an interior, you add vibrancy. However, if opposing colors are featured equally, the effect can be jarring, such as a red carpet and sofa in a bright blue-painted room.

If you are buying a range of new items for a room, you'll probably find that they share a common palette, and are in colors and tones that are currently popular across the board. However, upcycled pieces will often have been made in a different era, with different pigments or color compositions. This is why they often offer a good "pop" of contrast color or added vibrancy to a modern color scheme.

Opposite and above left: This end of the living room provides the color, with the bookcase, lamp, and chair offering a bright, uplifting contrast to the cool blues and grays. Tim drew the shelves where he wanted them to be on the wall and had the bookcase made to his exact specification. He painted the lamp using car spray paint. Behind the lamp is one of Tim's paintings—of the covers of some of the books in this very bookcase. The chair is from the 1950s, reupholstered in royal blue corduroy by designer Melissa North. All these pieces are in similar tones—in other words, they are as bright or as dark as each other, which is the reason why they work so well together.

Above: The 1950s saw an explosion in good design for everyday use, and new manufacturing techniques meant greater affordability, too. Houses then were built with lower ceilings—as they are today—so 1950s lighting, like these five pendant lights, works particularly well in modern homes.

This seating area at the end of the kitchen uses white paint and pale upholstery to maximize the light, with the odd pop of vibrant vintage color.

Upholstered furniture is perfect for upcycling. Many classic chair designs, such as the armchairs opposite, have been produced for nearly one hundred years and are still being manufactured. But buying such tailored pieces new comes with a hefty price tag. You can buy similar pieces cheaply from chain stores, although the quality is not as good—expect foam rather than sprung seats, for example. Luckily, upholstered furniture is often passed down to family or among friends. It can usually be bought quite inexpensively in auction rooms, too, and bargains can always be found on the internet. However, before you buy secondhand chairs and sofas online, quiz the vendor about their condition and take careful measurements. It's too easy to bid for a fabulous sofa and then find that it won't fit up the stairs or through the front door.

Having sofas and large chairs reupholstered can be quite expensive. The price of the material and the labor may mean that it works out about half of what such a piece of furniture would cost new. That's still good value for money, but not cheap.

Opposite: Secondhand, reupholstered chairs and an old wooden cupboard, painted white and placed in the space under the stairs, make Tim's sitting room an upcycler's dream. The vivid red in the Uzbek rug, which was a gift, is picked out in the spotted tea service that Tim collected piece by piece. Meanwhile, the pitcher (from Scarlet & Violet) and bowl of lemons counter with a splash of vivid yellow. The floorboards are from a school gymnasium.

Right: This wall art was put together by Tim from plastic color samples he found on a factory floor. They were to be thrown away, but he gathered them up and presented them in a box frame—upcycled art at its best.

new-build *hacks*

It's not just furniture that is mass-produced. New houses and apartments can also feel as if they have come out of a flat-pack catalog, especially if they've been built on a budget, and their kitchens and bathrooms are always standard. They're also often extremely short of space, especially storage space.

Shown here is the living area of writer Penny Rich's new-build apartment, at the other end of her kitchen (see page 30). Her main hack—and her biggest investment—was the white resin floor, which made the apartment much lighter and brighter.

She divided up the space using white, modular units bought from a chain store. In 4s, 8s and 16s, they are used as room dividers, cupboards, drawers, and display shelves, increasing the amount of storage as well as breaking up the single space that forms the kitchen and living area. Changing the handles on the doors and drawers has given them individuality, while choosing a gloss finish has maximized the amount of light.

Penny's furnishings are a mix of vintage and modern. She's made a small room feel lighter and larger by upcycling neat, stylish furniture from the 1950s and '60s, and reupholstering them in smart, contemporary fabrics. The 1950s teak dining table is by Danish designer Hans Olsen for Frem Rojle. It's extendable, while the matching chairs are stackable and also fit under the tabletop, saving even more space when not in use.

Opposite: The 1970s Parker Knoll Penshurst two-seater sofa takes up the minimum amount of space. Penny has transformed it by re-covering it in traditional embroidered suzani fabric from Uzbekistan. The English wing chair, from the 1950s, was found at a tailgate (car boot) sale. After sanding and oiling the wood, Penny reupholstered it in an eye-popping lime-green velvet. The vivid colors of these two pieces are in stark contrast to the gilt-framed painting from Penny's previous home and the wooden cabinet, creating a visual balance. The Holophane glass and aluminum ceiling light comes from a 1930s Ministry of Defence munitions factory in Wales. *Above:* The secondhand leather reclining chair is "very comfortable." At the window, a fretwork screen offers privacy but doesn't block the light.

Penny's white walls and floor are the perfect backdrop for colorful accessories. She loves trawling yard sales and flea markets. Her advice is to mix things up—vintage adds character to new things, and new gives vintage a different context in which it can shine.

Clockwise, from top left: A secondhand, woven plastic pinwheel footstool in orange and pink at the foot of a 1950s Danish armchair reupholstered in Designers Guild fabric; the wire and tops from champagne bottles fashioned into dolls' chairs; a vintage tin truck from Pakistan, painted in psychedelic colors; a "rag-rug" cushion unearthed at a "hippie store"; 1950s Danish chair, signed Ib Kofod-Larsen, re-covered in vintage-style fabric; classic crochet cushions chosen for their brilliant colors; glass ball doorknobs; vintage Huntley & Palmer cookie tins found at a tailgate (car boot) sale, now used as sewing boxes; a Murano glass vase bought in a closing-down sale; a Barbie doll chair; a vintage Czechoslovakian factory clock; "Love Love Love" felt cushion, hand-embroidered in wool, by Jan Constantine.

The different types of storage in Penny's apartment demonstrate her "mix it up" philosophy: new, chain-store modular storage units are combined with sloping bookshelves made to her specification, while an upcycled set of shelves displays her collection of vintage toys. "I was downsizing considerably, so I was desperate for cheap storage and I needed lots of it." With that in mind, she's combined drawers, cupboards, and open shelving, creating storage and display.

In a small space there are various ways of maximizing storage without making the room feel cluttered. Use the walls from floor to ceiling, as Penny has done, so that not an inch of space is wasted. A continuous run of units will also feel more spacious than several different types that divide up the wall. When furnishing smaller rooms, the general principle is that a few large pieces will work better than several small ones, because they will end up making a room look cluttered. Don't fall into the temptation of thinking "small room, small storage."

The color of your storage also contributes to the feeling of space. Penny has modern, upcycled, and tailor-made pieces, but she has kept the modern and the tailor-made white, so that they "disappear" into the white walls and floor, increasing the feeling of spaciousness and keeping the look streamlined.

Having floor, ceiling, and walls all painted bright white also increases the feeling of space. Painting rooms in one color on the walls and a contrasting color on the woodwork—doors, shelving, baseboards (skirting boards), carpets, dado rails, picture rails—breaks up the space visually and adds interest, but the more contrast there is, the less spacious it will feel.

Accurate measurements and careful planning are the key to effective storage. Storage should always be something that you consider at the outset. If you're redecorating a room, plan it at the same time as you choose the paint color. Be realistic when working out how much you need—don't just put cupboards and shelves wherever you can on the principle that you will always be able to fill them. And be flexible on the sizes of cupboards and shelves—there's not much point in having a cupboard where three-quarters of the space remains unused because the shelves are positioned too far apart.

Opposite: The sloping bookshelves are quirky and original. Penny designed them herself, taping out the shape she wanted on the wall after measuring her books so she knew they would fit. She employed a carpenter on a day rate to construct the unit, which she then painted white, helping to keep costs down. Poised above the upcycled shelves is an early nineteenth-century wooden fish from the South Pacific. "The zigzag of the bookshelf fitted the barracuda nose very well," says Penny.

Above: Penny bought a large quantity of inexpensive glass ball doorknobs from a hardware store and fitted them to the cupboards and drawers on the modular unit. A simple touch like this adds character to a chain-store purchase. Against this modern wall, her 1950s junk-shop furniture finds, updated with modern materials, look smart and contemporary.

Many patterns—checks, tartans, paisleys, and florals—have been produced for hundreds of years, while traditional Persian rug designs date as far back as the 5th century BC. So how do we use these styles and patterns in a fresh, contemporary way?

upcycling *pattern*

This living room belongs to artist Lucy Dickens, who paints scenes of her local Norfolk countryside. With her artist's eye for color, she has transformed shabby old furniture and discarded boxes to help create a delightful living room that's brimming over with character.

The best way to use traditional pattern without it looking dated is to mix things up. Combine pattern with plain, antique with contemporary. For example, if you have an antique Persian rug with a beautiful, elaborate pattern, show it off against plain white walls. Painting a traditional piece of furniture in a bright, modern color also works well, as with the yellow table.

Lucy re-covered the seat cushions on the secondhand sofa using an old checked coat, which has helped to prolong the sofa's life. Fire-retardant sprays that don't leave marks are available for most fabrics, but check local fire regulations before embarking on such a project yourself.

Above, from left to right: The coffee table is made up of the base of an old laundry cart and a wooden fruit crate. The yellow-painted side table is an old "cricket table". These three-legged stools, used in cottages from the seventeenth century, had only three legs, to make them more stable on uneven stone or earth floors. A bright red vintage toy train makes an eye-catching doorstop against the patterned rug.

Opposite: Traditional carpet patterns and checks look fresh and contemporary against a plain background. This sofa had cheap Crimplene seat cushions when Lucy first bought it. She has since re-covered them in material cut from an old coat. Re-covering cushions is relatively cheap and easy, compared to reupholstering an entire sofa.

a magpie *eye*

When writer and pop-up caterer Helen Frame and her partner Lee Shale decided to move from London to Somerset and live in the country, they found a 1710 row (terrace) house that had been "lovingly restored" by its previous owners. "We didn't want to change anything—we just moved in."

At first glance, their living room, with its silk and velvet furnishings, gives the impression of somewhere much grander. However, the sofa is a basic buy from a chain store, as are the luxurious-looking velvet cushions. Most of the remaining pieces hail from flea markets.

Helen and Lee run a mobile pop-up catering company, called Claud the Butler, from a vintage Citroën van. Whenever Helen delivers her home-made cakes to be sold at her local flea market, she never returns home empty-handed—she says she has a "magpie eye." All the decorative details in her home are reminders of a particular time, person, or event, such as the silver pot shown on the shelf opposite, which is a well-loved housewarming present from her children.

Above: Even though the look is sumptuous, the sofa, as well as the velvet scatter cushions, are inexpensive purchases from chain stores. The sheepskin throw is from a local store—Somerset, where Helen and Lee live, is well known for its sheep—and the other throws were collected while on vacation. One came from a little boutique in France.

Opposite: The abstract painting was a gift from an artist friend, Anthony Daley. The hydrangeas are displayed in an old zinc florists' bucket.

Overleaf left: Helen says that virtually everything in her home has a memory attached to it. She bought the little yellow pitcher, filled with roses, in a market in Provence, and it stands as a constant reminder of a lovely vacation. The slender vase on the left, which she fell in love with in a local store, is made of wood. The one on the right is Murano glass—a cherished gift.

Overleaf right: The little leather armchair came from the local flea market. Helen spotted it when she was delivering cakes.

Helen describes the interior of their home as "a mix of our London life and our new one—there are things I bought at Portobello Market in London, and from the local fleamarket in Frome."

The two of us have written a number of books covering fleamarket shopping, and we sometimes get comments such as, "I never find anything so nice when I go to a fleamarket," or "Whenever I see things like that, they're always very expensive." To develop a magpie eye like Helen takes time, and finding exactly the piece you want can take years. It helps, whenever you have a moment, to wander around local markets or junk shops, to "get your eye in." You are then more likely to spot a bargain, often in a corner, covered in dust.

And if you are after something specific, such as pretty, French garden chairs, then look at as many as you can—in stores, online, and in magazines. The more you know about an item, the easier it will be to recognize a good version of it. You'll also find out more about what you might be expected to pay—and don't forget to add in the cost of transportation, if necessary.

Opposite: The elegant French garden chair is one of four that Helen found in a London junk shop. The shapely table, also French, complements it perfectly. Not everything Helen buys is secondhand. The pretty lamp comes from an upmarket accessories store in the Portobello Road, London. Spending money on gorgeous decorative touches can lift junk-shop furniture beautifully.

Above left: Helen bought the square of stained glass as a sample from a stained-glass artist in a local craft center —she was hoping to replace a square of glass missing from a door. Sadly, when she returned, the artist had left and no one knew her name.

Above center: Now displayed on the stone mantelpiece, the vintage floral teacup with its matching saucer is one of many that Helen has collected for the pop-up catering business that she and Lee run from a vintage Citroën van.

Above right: A squat, metal candle-holder from London's Portobello Road market complements the hammered silver pot, given as a housewarming present by Helen's children.

sparkle *and drama*

Movie and stage sets used to be dismantled and thrown away at the end of a production, but now there are green initiatives in the arts world, too, encouraging people to recycle rather than throw everything into landfill. However, recycled stage props are still not yet widely available, and even looking for them on the internet can be a frustrating business. There are, though, a number of green arts organizations and stage prop recycling charities and directories that have been set up to help people find secondhand props (see pages 156–157).

The living room featured here belongs to actress Joanne McQuinn, and she is sometimes lucky enough to buy pieces from a set. She made the striking side table shown opposite from two plaster capitals (the tops of classical columns), turning one upside down on top of the other, and adding a framed mirror for the tabletop.

Joanne also makes use of festive decorations at home to add light, color, and sparkle throughout the year. Like her, you could hang baubles in front of mirrors, from ceilings, or window frames. And wind garlands of lights across the top of a bookcase, or around windows, pictures, mirrors, or mantelpieces. They also look good curled up inside glass vases.

Above left: The romantic lampshade on top of the side table, once a stage prop comprising two architectural capitals and a mirror, was made from a vintage tablecloth, by Fein & Cooper.

Above: Joanne bought the Art-Deco-style velvet sofa and two armchairs from an antique store for a few hundred pounds—a set like this would usually cost at least a thousand.

Opposite: The vintage armchair is one of a pair Joanne bought from a friend who was going to live abroad. It was originally covered in chintz but its current white slipcover gives it a more contemporary look. The fuchsia-pink mohair throw adds a touch of glamour. Reflected in the mirror above the sideboard are the large purple baubles that Joanne has hung from the ceiling, which she felt was too low. The light reflecting off them helps to lift the atmosphere. The pretty garland of fairy lights from India, draped around the mirror, performs a similar role.

everything *has a story*

This is Mark and Talya Rochester's living room. The Edwardian sofa—a beautiful, traditional piece of furniture in a classic design—has been re-covered and a woolen, fringed throw added for extra comfort.

Mark finds the furniture for both his business (upcycling and selling vintage furniture) and for his home at a number of different places, including schools, hospitals, factories, and even parking lots, or—as the fire bucket above shows—the British Museum in London. He knows a great deal about where vintage industrial fixtures and fittings were made, and everything featured on the Rochester's website (see page 156) is accompanied by a story of how it was found. Mark loves being surrounded by things that "have had a life before," although, ultimately, they have to be practical as well. This they mostly are, although he says that Talya does sometimes find the factory chairs less comfortable than modern ones.

Above left: The shutters are made from pottery boards—planks of wood where pots were set out to dry. Some boards have the names of individual potters scratched on them.

Above: An old fire-bucket from the British Museum is an evocative container for fire irons, while a large industrial container is used for kindling.

Opposite: The portrait of the racing pigeon was painted by E.H. Windred in the 1930s, one of many that he did of race-winners as prizes for their owners. The chest came from a drugstore in Wales.

Overleaf: The long draper's table is used as a desk and work station. The blackboard came from an Edwardian school, and the chairs are factory or mill chairs from the same period.

Many people collect industrial implements, such as antique mathematical instruments, scientific gauges, or old laboratory equipment, simply because such things are often surprisingly beautiful or interesting. Many of the items shown here could form a wonderful collection—they are memories of a working way of life that by and large has disappeared.

Clockwise, from top left: Letters from an old card game called Lexicon; a photography light from the 1940s or '50s; a colorful stuffed parakeet; the seat of an early Singer sewing chair without its back, now used as a stool; a vintage wooden mathematical compass; a 1920s Dugdill articulating desk lamp, made of brass, for use in studios, workshops, and factories; a Victorian butterfly collection, with the colors still remarkably bright; a Toledo chair, made in the early twentieth century in the U.S. for draftsmen; a 1920s, illuminated eye-test chart from the U.S.; blocks for making up price stamps in U.K. stores before the currency was decimalized in 1971; a Singer sewing machine chair, used in an early twentieth-century garment factory; an anatomical model from a French medical school dating from around 1900.

chapter three
bedrooms

Sanctuary and storage—these are the two words that sum up your bedroom. It's both an intensely personal space and one that has to function well. The biggest expenditure is your bed. You can find some good bargains by buying ex-hotel beds —"bedroom sets," complete with side tables, desks and sometimes even lights, are particularly good value. Search on the internet for "secondhand hotel beds" or "ex-contract furniture." You can also hack a new bed by buying the frame or divan and mattress, then adding a recycled or tailor-made headboard. When it comes to the rest of the bedroom furniture—chairs, bedside tables, storage, and so on—there are lots of good ideas in the following pages.

The Victorian-style bedroom, with its cast-iron bedstead and patchwork counterpane, is ideal for upcyclers, as bedside chests and cabinets don't need to match, and vintage lighting suits the atmosphere. The key to looking contemporary rather than cluttered is to keep it simple, taking your time to find each item and choosing only those that you really love.

modern *Victoriana*

This bedroom, in the attic of a Victorian house, belongs to actress Joanne McQuinn. It originally had a flat ceiling but Joanne created a sense of space by taking this out and exposing the slope of the roof. She also removed fitted cupboards, behind which she found original plaster. She loved this surface so much that she decided not to paint it—just protect it with varnish.

Victorian brass bed frames used to be picked up for next to nothing, but they have become so popular that you may not find any bargains. Ensure that they are sound—wiggle the frame, and check iron parts for rust. Check measurements, too—a hundred years ago, people were smaller. Most people prefer to have a new mattress, as old mattresses can harbor bed bugs and be lumpy and uncomfortable. Some countries have regulations on how old mattresses must be professionally cleaned—but not everyone sticks to them!

Above left: Instead of one central light, Joanne has three pendant lights with vintage glass shades, each slightly different—one might have looked a little too small in the space, while a larger, central ceiling light could have been rather overwhelming.

Above center: Joanne makes lampshades from old silk scarves, because the silk casts such a beautiful light.

Above right: The Victorian brass bed was an inexpensive purchase at an auction house.

Opposite: The bedside cabinet was left behind in a previous house that Joanne lived in. "Brown furniture" is at its least popular at the moment, meaning that practical, pretty little pieces like this are often almost given away.

It's the simplicity of the color scheme that makes this room seem so contemporary, even though the furniture in it is Victorian. The picture opposite shows the other end of the room featured on the previous pages: an attic space with a sloping roof and old-fashioned, wooden floorboards. The tongue-and-groove boarding around the window and gable end is suitably humble for an attic—such rooms were originally built either as servants' bedrooms or for storage. Grandeur would seem out of place.

If your attic or roof space is not yet converted, you could consider "upcycling" it yourself and turning it into more living space. However, each country has very specific regulations as to what it will allow—most will require that there is already enough height to stand and move about easily, as you're unlikely to be able to raise the height of the roof. You will also have to comply with rules about the way the staircase is placed, and you'll probably need to increase both insulation and ventilation. When costing out a loft conversion, find out what the average property price per square foot or meter is in your area. A loft conversion will undoubtedly give you more living space, but you need to know that you are not paying over the odds for it.

Opposite: The sloping roof of the attic bedroom featured on the previous pages is clearly visible in this view from the other end of the room. The slipcovered armchair is one of a pair—its partner is downstairs in the living room (see page 71).

Above right: A simple, red-spotted lace panel is pinned to the window, creating privacy but also allowing the light through. You don't need very much material for this kind of treatment—look for remnants in fabric stores during their sales.

Right: There is a very contemporary use of color and pattern in this bedroom. Against the calm, neutral backdrop there is just the occasional Victorian motif, like this posy on the ceramic ball on the footboard.

bedroom *hacks*

This is the bedroom of writer Penny Rich. The apartment was brand new when she moved in—a blank canvas with small rooms and no storage. In Penny's living room (see pages 56–61), she has used chain-store, modular storage units in white as room dividers and also for display. Here, she continues the theme, creating a dressing area with cupboards and shelves.

This kind of modern storage makes a better use of space than free-standing cupboards. By painting the walls white—the same color as the units—she's achieved a sleek, contemporary look in what is a small space containing a great number of things.

Chain-store storage units like these can be used in the bedroom as the base for a bed, seating, a desk, or a table. To give them your own personal stamp, change any handles—Penny used glass ball doorknobs for her drawers and cupboard doors—or add or change the legs, either to make the units the right height for their intended use, or simply to make them look a little bit different. Decorating the doors will also set them apart, as will painting the whole unit. Although modular units like these are usually laminated or varnished, there are primer paints available that are specially designed for this purpose.

Opposite: Penny has created a "dressing room" area behind her bed, stacked high with floor-to-ceiling cupboards and shelves. On one side, a unit acts as the headboard for her bed; on the other, there are drawers. Open shelves display her favorite things, and the side of the cupboards creates "wall space" for hanging paintings. The stripy bedlinen is from a homewares chain store.

Right: The "dressing room" side of the storage units shows them used as shelves, drawers, and cupboards. Penny bought a large number of inexpensive glass ball doorknobs from a hardware store to personalize the units.

hand-me-down *chic*

Opposite: Joanne bought this Victorian metal bed very cheaply because it was missing a side bar, but she then commissioned a metalworker to fit it with a side bar from another damaged bed. A wooden chair with a flat seat makes a good bedside table, and it will be easy to repaint if Joanne's daughter decides she would like a different color scheme. The curtains are a pair of French bedspreads. Joanne is very creative about using fabrics in different ways from how they were originally intended. On page 47, you can see how she has used a curtain as a table runner.

Above, left to right: A pretty garland of fake flowers adds a splash of color. Don't just use bunting for special occasions —it will add atmosphere and gaiety at any time. The curtains made from bedspreads are hung with inexpensive, chain-store curtain rings and are simply clipped on, making it quick and easy to take them down.

This bedroom belongs to Joanne McQuinn's' 11-year-old daughter. It shows that you shouldn't have any preconceived ideas about how to decorate a child's room—there's no need to have pink or blue themes, or go the fairies/ballerinas/train engines route. Everything here is upcycled or recycled, with a bedroom chair adapted as a bedside table, and a broken Victorian bed repaired and ready for use again.

The advantage of recycled and upcycled furniture for children's rooms is that anything that has survived so far will probably be fairly sturdy. And if it already looks battered, then it doesn't matter if a few more marks appear. Buying cheap, modern furniture and hacking it also works—if it doesn't cost a great deal to decorate your child's room, that gives you much more flexibility to change it more regularly as they grow and their tastes change.

The main issue is safety. Check that any secondhand furniture really is sound—that the joints of tables, chairs, and beds are secure and don't wobble. Wood should be smooth and not liable to splinter. And if you have vintage toys with breakable parts, such as dolls with china heads, then make sure that very young children don't play with them unsupervised.

Once all these things have been checked, there is a great satisfaction in giving your child furniture and toys that are part of a history, especially when it is your own family's history.

These pictures show other views of the bedroom featured on pages 86–7. It is furnished with an antique wooden armoire and chest of drawers. Nineteenth- and twentieth-century wooden furniture is now referred to—somewhat disparagingly—as "brown furniture." Its popularity and price have dipped sharply over the last decade or so as trends have moved toward contemporary interiors, but it offers superb value for money. It's also often made from hardwoods, such as mahogany, oak, or walnut. It would be expensive to get furniture made in these types of wood today.

Many antique stores selling similar vintage wooden furniture no longer exist, so the market has moved online. Look, too, in auction rooms and estate sale shops (house clearance sales).

Above left: Joanne stripped the wallpaper on the chimney breast back to reveal the original plaster, which she loved. She then varnished it so she could continue to enjoy its texture and mottled colors. The armchair is a twentieth-century Sanderson chair, in its original upholstery—when Joanne bought it, it had a loose cover, which she removed.

Above: Sitting on the mantelpiece is an antique mirror surrounded by Indian fairy lights, made in a delicate leaf design. Tucked behind the frame is a favorite postcard from Amsterdam.

Opposite: The armoire and the chest of drawers, bought from an estate sale shop (house clearance sale), have a beautiful patina that would not be found in new pieces of furniture.

young *upcycling*

This bedroom belongs to our youngest upcycler, Minna Ford, aged 13, who has been buying things at rummage sales and thrift stores since she was seven years old. "And if there's something no one's using around the house, then I ask if I can have it," she says.

Most of Minna's pictures are stuck to the wall with reusable adhesive, including the vinyl LP she found in a thrift store. "It fell to the ground and chipped, but I like it with jagged edges." Some of the postcards on the wall have been sent to the family, but Minna bought the majority of them. She asked for the all-in-one antique school desk and chair as a birthday gift. It's where she does her homework.

Opposite: The child-size sofa was Minna's crib when she was a baby. It came from a furniture chain store, and has now had one side removed and has been painted. The seat cushion is covered with an old curtain. Minna's mother gave new life to the table by stapling oilcloth to the top and painting the legs. The little cabinet on top of the chest of drawers belonged to her grandmother. Minna cut out the pictures above from vintage Butterick sewing patterns.

Right: Minna bought the flower painting at a rummage sale when she was seven. The poster of the head is wrapping paper—a birthday present from her brother—and the sneakers were an upcycled present from her friend Tallulah, who tie-dyed them pink.

blue and white *simplicity*

Simplicity works beautifully with upcycling and recycling. A room with white walls and a restrained use of color—as with the blue and white scheme shown here—really shows off the shape, patina, and texture of vintage objects. It's the difference between cluttered and contemporary.

The most decorative piece of furniture in this bedroom is the blue-painted chair from Eastern Europe, featuring a sweet little folk-art emblem on the seat back. Since the collapse of the Soviet Union, there has been increasing interest in traditional folk art and painted furniture from countries formerly part of the Soviet bloc. There are dealers in the US, UK, and Europe who specialize in such furniture and make trips to Eastern Europe, returning with benches, settles, chairs, and other miscellanous items. You can, of course, travel there and do the buying yourself, although you may find it difficult to find authentic folk furniture—flea markets in the bigger cities are now mainly aimed at tourists. However, you can still pick up delightful pieces in the countryside at very reasonable prices—look for the timeless folk designs that remind you of traditional fairy tales.

Above left: An old kitchen shelf displays a vintage horse and cart, and a framed picture of Charles Dickens' original shorthand notes given to his great-grandchildren. The Eastern European chair came from an antique store in England. Its shape, color, and folk-art design are typical of traditional, pre-Soviet era furniture.

Above: The closet is original to the house. Although it isn't as deep as today's modern, fitted cupboards, it has the advantage of being much less obtrusive.

Opposite: An English Victorian cast-iron bed is covered with a traditional blue-and-white Welsh blanket—plaids and checks are the most common pattern for Welsh blankets, but you can also find tapestry designs. There were also a lot of Welsh blankets produced in the 1950s, '60s, and '70s in more modernist patterns, which are equally charming. Look for blankets made of real wool—but guard against moths.

Clockwise, from top left: A pair of watercolors by the English artist Mary Fedden; a close-up of the folk-art detail on the Eastern European chair in the bedroom; a vintage cream cup—without its saucer—makes a charming vase for a posy of hellebores; a 1920s glass lampshade; feathers instead of flowers in a glass jar; a kitchen shelf is repurposed for the bedroom—the row of hooks is very useful for hanging clothes; an antique wooden toy is given a new role as a doorstop; a Welsh blanket in a traditional plaid pattern; an old toy horse which was once a child's treasured pull-along toy; a French garden table is repurposed as a bedside table—the edge of the table is made of horn; upcycling means mixing simplicity with more ornate things—here, a humble enamel candle holder works well with an ornate antique mirror.

Overleaf left: Bedside tables don't have to match. Here, an unusual French garden table finds a new use as a bedroom side table.

Overleaf right: This kitchen shelf was moved into the bedroom, offering a charming opportunity to display some treasured possessions: an old toy horse and cart, a folk-art tapestry, and a page taken from one of Charles Dickens' shorthand notebooks.

color *highlights*

The use of color is important in upcycling and hacking because it can pull everything together. An upcycled interior will usually have things from lots of different eras—Victorian, 1920s, 1970s and present day, for example. Using a limited color palette, such as red and white, makes the effect crisp and contemporary rather than muddled. This is another white-based scheme, which uses a good, strong red as the highlight color—in the bedspreads, the lamp on the chest of drawers, and the pattern on the chest.

The chest of drawers was bought as a flat-pack from a chain store. It has been painted white, and wrapping paper has been glued onto the drawer fronts—a very cheap hack indeed. And in case you think that such a treatment will look shabby after a very short time, we did a similar hack on a chest of drawers for a book we were writing together in 1994. It is still in use today, only slightly battered-looking.

Above: Metal-frame school beds from a junk shop. Such beds were produced in their thousands when Britain's Empire meant that many children were sent away to private schools. The bedspreads are from India, the unusual double, vintage lamp from a chain store.

Opposite: This modern, chain-store chest of drawers has been made unique by gluing wrapping paper to the drawers and adding new handles. Antique mirrors like this are usually gilded, but silver leaf is just as beautiful and looks more contemporary. Gilding with silver, gold, or copper leaf is a fairly skilled job, so don't start with an ambitious project—start with something small. The orange lamp came from Marianna Kennedy.

go with *what you've got*

Both bedrooms featured on these two pages contain elements you might be tempted to cover up or rip out, but, instead, the owners have incorporated them.

Take cupboards, for example. You may buy a home where previous owners have fitted cupboards everywhere. Removing all or some of them will undoubtedly make rooms feel more spacious. However, there may be some that are an intrinsic part of the architecture of the house. This was the case with the bedroom shown on the right in artist Thomasina Smith's home. She has retained the original closet, including the interior mirror and tie rack, that came with the house. However, she has upcycled it by painting the doors with her "take on Charleston." Charleston was Virginia Woolf's home, famous for its hand-painted finishes, and Thomasina worked as a painter on the set of *The Hours*, the movie based on Woolf's *Mrs Dalloway*.

Opposite: Instead of covering over the open ceiling in his bedroom, artist Tim Braden has minimized its impact by painting it white, which still keeps the extra height that it provides and also adds to the room's character. The bed, covered with a Celia Birtwell fabric, is from an antique store. Standing a big mirror on the floor works well in bedrooms—it's easier to see yourself full-length.

Right: The cupboards were built in with the house, which dates from the 1920s. Thomasina painted these closet doors in "Charleston" colors with a little elephant emblem, but uses the original interior fittings. Painting cupboards also works well if you're hacking flat-pack furniture—even laminates can be painted as long as you use the right primer. The wooden rocking horse came from an antique store.

recycling *school*

This bedroom belongs to vintage furniture dealer Mark Rochester and his artist wife, Talya Baldwin. As in the rest of their house, everything has come from somewhere else and has a history. Several items were from an old school gym that was being refurbished. Even those who hated gymnastics in their schooldays have to admit that the equipment in older schools was often made of beautiful wood, and that school gym floors were often the envy of any ballroom.

Old school lockers, gym and swimming pool lockers, and sports club lockers have all become eagerly sought after by recyclers and upcyclers. Usually made of wire or metal, they are being turned into cabinets, clothes storage, or chests, or simply left as lockers. You can either spray-paint them or let them keep their nicely battered vintage look. In the bedroom featured here, a narrow stack of wire gym lockers fits perfectly into the recess created by the chimney breast, offering useful storage.

You can also incorporate old doors or shutters into storage. Using shutters that were originally in a theater for the doors, Mark had a carpenter build a cupboard flush with the chimney breast on the other side for a streamlined effect.

Above left: You can just see the stack of wire gym baskets used to store clothes on the left-hand side of the chimney breast. The metal chair is an old French garden chair. Garden furniture often works well inside the home, although make sure that the metal feet won't damage your flooring.
Left: This unusual chair from a Methodist chapel makes the perfect bedside table. Underneath the hinged seat, there is valuable storage space.
Opposite: Taking advantage of the recess created by the chimney breast, Mark had a cupbard built, using Victorian theater shutters for the doors.

Those with depressing memories of chilly gym sessions in dusty halls will remember the gym bars shown opposite—known as monkey bars—with no great affection. But vintage school gymnasium equipment is becoming increasingly sought-after.

In Mark and Talya's bedroom, the wall bars make great storage for shoes, but they would work just as well for ties, scarves, hats—or even for pots and pans in the kitchen. Other pieces of vintage school equipment now being recycled and upcycled include pommel horses, made of well-worn leather and wood. They have been spotted in smart cafés, used as a bar on which to rest your coffee. Similarly, antique gym benches blend perfectly into family life without needing any adaptation.

Above left and above: Artist Thomasina Smith paints standard pieces of furniture with patterns inspired by vintage fabric and wallpaper. This design is based on an old French wallpaper. It's almost too beautiful to be called a "hack."

Opposite: School gymnasium bars from the 1920s make unusual but practical bedroom storage. The chair is an early twentieth-century French café chair made by Xavier Pauchard, who was the first man in France to produce galvanized metal furniture. Impervious to rust, Pauchard chairs were produced in their thousands. They are now style icons, but many for sale are replica, repro, or "Pauchard-style."

historical *romance*

When Victorian style had its great revival in the 1980s and '90s, period style was assumed to be cluttered and frilly, with swags, flounces, and ornaments. However, the real key to historical style is simplicity. It wasn't until after the Industrial Revolution, in Victorian times, that the consumer society as we know it was created. Before that, only the very wealthiest people owned more than the bare necessities, so most homes were simple and quite spartan, with relatively little storage required.

Shown here is one of the bedrooms in the home of Helen Frame and Lee Shale. As soon as they viewed the house, the previous owners gave them details of its history. It was built as one of four row (terrace) houses, for cloth merchants in the eighteenth century, during Queen Anne's reign. These merchants would have been reasonably well-off, but in those days, upcycling was the norm for practically everyone—when a new house was built, beams, doors, and paneling were often taken from houses about to be demolished and reused.

Downstairs rooms used for entertaining were always fitted with architectural elements of a much higher quality than those in the bedrooms. Upstairs, old doors, latches, and tongue-and-groove paneling, as shown here, would only be seen by the family and their servants, rather than by guests.

Opposite: Bedrooms in older houses often have simple, almost rustic doors, which may even have been upcycled themselves from previous buildings. Lee brought the little bedside table stool back from a cycling trip in Burma. Helen collects old bedlinen, and the simple wooden bed is made up with vintage linen sheets from a market in Provence.

Above right: Clothes will have hung on a hook on the back of this door for three hundred years. This pretty, lace-edged camisole is displayed on one of the padded coat hangers in Helen's collection.

Right: A chain-store embroidered pillowcase complements the vintage candy-stripe one underneath.

Far right: Helen also collects china pitchers, which she sometimes uses for milk, at other times for flowers.

a sense of *time and place*

Upcycling adds texture and pattern to a home. It's not just the style of older furniture that makes a home look distinctive, but also the patina of age that these pieces bring—the sense that they have been lived with and loved for a long time. Nothing is quite perfect, but everything tells a story.

In the main bedroom of this historic house, Helen has added restrained elements of colour and texture, so that the architecture can really be enjoyed without the distraction of excessive furnishings. At the time that this house was built, the furnishings would often have been secondhand or passed down through the generations, so upcycling suits it well. But even if you live in a modern home, you can still give it a sense of time and place by buying pieces for it that have been made locally or finding things that reflect your life and character.

An antique headboard is a stylish way of adding color and texture to a plain bedroom. If you find one that doesn't fit your bed exactly, you can usually modify it or attach it to the wall rather than to the bed. You may want to think twice about having a footboard—if you are tall, or if you watch television in bed, it may not be at all comfortable.

Opposite left: The antique green velvet headboard and footboard were "a nice little find," says Helen. "There's a local shop I often pop into, and I spotted them shoved into a corner, so I bought them."

Opposite right: Helen had intended to hang a collection of mirrors on the bathroom wall. With that in mind, she bought several at her local fleamarket. "In the end, I decided against it, so I've propped them up around the house in various places. The necklaces are bits and bobs I've collected all my life. The little bowl was a present from a friend, and the sequin purse was a present from my daughter."

Above left: Helen and Lee's house was originally restored by artist and former museum curator, Chris Bucklow, who paid close attention to re-creating historical accuracy. He painted this "ghostly paneling" on the bedroom walls—an echo of what would have been. Helen bought the Berber rugs in Morocco—Middle Eastern rugs have been adorning homes in the West for centuries.

Above right: This 1950s Chinese-style paper lantern just appealed to Helen. It looks pretty hanging from a doorknob and reminds her of the rummage sales of her childhood. "I used to love going to local sales, and spotting something sitting, covered in dust, under a pile of things."

Objets *trouvés*, or found objects, are at the heart of upcycling. They can cost you nothing or be almost free: a postcard, pages torn from a magazine, a secondhand book, Christmas decorations, old bottles used as vases… and, as you rummage in junk shops and thrift stores, start to look at things differently. What about that lamp that reminds you of your grandparents' house? You thought it was hideous in their home, but in a different context, you can see its appeal.

Don't throw things away without a second thought—reuse them. A slightly chipped glass that can't be used for drinking can become a vase for flowers, and a leaky pitcher or pot can be planted up with plants and spend its final days outdoors, although it might not survive the winter. There are many, many more new uses to give to things that can no longer do the job they were meant for. Above all, if you've become tired of something or don't have room for it any more, sell it or give it away.

Above left: Helen collects postcards and uses them as decoration, alongside a mercury-glass tea light holder and a scented candle in a vintage cup and saucer. "I often use old china cups for tea lights because they give off a lovely glow," she says.

Above: The lamp on the French garden chair dates from the 1960s—it's just the sort of unfashionable lamp to be found cheaply in rummage sales.

Opposite: The fireplace is covered by a screen made from pages torn from a copy of *Vogue*: "When I see a fashion shoot that I really like, I often tear it out and pin it up," says Helen. The chair is from a thrift store.

chapter four

bathrooms

When you're shopping for bathroom fittings, what at first looks like a bewildering amount of choice ends with the realization that every brochure carries a variation on only about three different styles and that your bathroom is likely to look exactly like everyone else's. To give your bathroom personality, try a few upcycling and hacking tricks. You could introduce one vintage element, such as a stunning mirror or a claw-foot bathtub, to a very modern bathroom, or drop a conventional basin into a secondhand piece of furniture. Another way is to use tiling and paint to make a standard chain-store bathroom something special—see these pages for inspiration.

mix old *and new*

Practicality has to come before personality when you're planning a bathroom, but once you've worked out the best positioning for bathtub, basin, shower, and toilet, then you can enjoy the decorating. Bathrooms are often the smallest rooms in the house and they take only a small amount of something special to create atmosphere and add color. If you don't have the budget to replace existing fittings, adding your own personal touches need not be costly or even time-consuming.

Both bathrooms featured on these two pages are fitted with standard modern units. To lift the scheme of her bathroom, shown left, artist Lucy Dickens has used paint, while for the bathroom opposite, actress Joanne McQuinn has introduced small amounts of luxurious materials, such as marble and colorful patterned tiles.

Marble has always spelt luxury and wealth. Using it sparingly won't cost a great deal yet it will transform the appearance of a small bathroom. You can find reclaimed marble surprisingly cheaply online—sometimes people advertise old worktops or surplus slabs of marble for sale. Check that the marble is suitable for bathrooms, though—some types are marked more easily, for example with hair dye, fake tanning lotions, or harsh cleaning products.

Opposite: Marble wall tiles and cement "patchwork" floor tiles from Emery et Cie make Joanne's bathroom look special. Emery et Cie sell these tiles in a random box. It's cheaper than buying their specific patterns but you won't know what you've bought until you open the box.

Above and above left: After the walls were tiled, there was enough leftover marble to make a bathroom shelf. You could also source small off-cuts of granite, stone and resin surfaces to make shelving.

backsplashes *and flooring*

If you want to upcycle or hack a regular bathroom, then changing the tiling or flooring is often one of the cheapest ways of creating an impact. These pictures of Joanne McQuinn's shower room show pretty, colorful tiles adorning both the basin backsplash and the floor.

If you're tiling only a small area, then you might decide to invest in a few expensive tiles. It can be worth checking in tile stores for ends of lines, which are often available at highly discounted prices. You can take the same approach with other expensive floorings, such as luxury vinyl floor coverings or carpet.

Some tiles wear better on floors than others. Porcelain and cement tiles are both more water-resistant than ceramic or marble tiles, and for that reason are considered better choices for bathroom floors. The tiles that Joanne has used for her bathroom floor are made of cement and can also be used outdoors.

Above left: Joanne has used enameled terracotta zelig tiles in a gorgeous turquoise from Emery et Cie for the small backsplash above the basin. The decorative framed mirror is a pretty alternative to the average bathroom mirror.

Above and opposite: Patchwork tiling can be very attractive—and you don't necessarily have to use all the same sorts of tiles. Mix a few expensive favorites in among more standard ones or edge a design of basic tiles with those that are more special. For a large area, such as a shower, cheaper tiles could be used for the wall, while reserving the more expensive ones for something smaller, like a basin backsplash.

You can turn a bathroom into a mini gallery, even if your room is very small or utilitarian, adding personality with a row of special tiles, or collections of pictures, plates, shells, or toys.

Above: Artist Thomasina Smith applied a sticky-backed gel, generally used on store windows, to windows in her bathroom, in order to increase privacy.

Above left: Thomasina uses pictures, including one drawn by her young daughter, to distract from the ventilation unit. The tiles beneath the fleamarket mirror are from the 1930s.

Opposite above: On either side of the sink, there are two pieces of marble inset — you can find small off-cuts of marble quite cheaply.

Opposite below: You can use china dishes or shells as soap-dishes, and pretty jugs, pitchers, or mugs for toothbrushes—you don't have to be restricted by accessories made specifically for bathrooms.

bathroom *details*

Bathrooms don't need to be stark and without decoration. They're an excellent space for hanging pictures, which are easier to see closeup in what is often a small space. You can create a collage, display children's paintings, or hang china plates or a collection of pretty mirrors—one big statement piece reflected in them will create a wow factor.

There are a few practical considerations, however. Space will usually be tight, so hang your displays where they won't be knocked every time you open a cabinet door, for example. Remember, too, that sprays, such as perfume and hairspray, are often used in the bathroom, so any artwork needs to be protected behind glass.

Then there is the damage that moisture can cause to pictures. Although today's bathrooms and shower rooms are fitted with ventilation and heating systems, some moisture can still seep underneath conventional frames over time. To prevent this, there are "weatherproof" or "waterproof" picture frames available (these were originally made for gardens or graveyards). Also, a professional framer will be able to frame your pictures to help protect them from the effects of condensation. Alternatively, you could just take the risk, as I have—I've always had pictures on the walls of my small shower rooms and bathrooms, and the only water damage ever caused was to one that I hung in the actual shower cubicle!

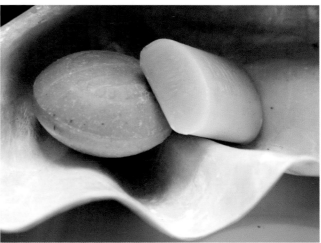

contemporary *classics*

Mixing new purchases with upcycled ones can be approached in a variety of ways. One option when buying new is to choose pieces in classic styles. The definition of "classic" is something that has a timeless quality. Classic pieces always look current, regardless of context, and mix well with all design eras. For example, a bathtub, basin, or faucets (taps) that were originally designed in, say, the 1920s but still look right in today's homes, would be considered classics. "Vintage," on the other hand, means old or from a particular time, usually the twentieth century. Consequently, vintage pieces are less versatile.

The bathroom featured here belongs to artist and sculptor Tim Braden. Most of the furniture and fittings in his home are upcycled, which meant that there wasn't any specific architectural style that needed to be followed for the bathroom fittings. But, as classic style usually works with anything, he chose classic styles of bathtub, basin, and radiator. The result, combined with a smattering of fleamarket finds, is both contemporary and stylish.

Opposite: The classic basin and bathtub were bought from a major bathroom retailer. An advantage of fitting recently manufactured sanitary ware is that you don't have to worry about whether modern pipework will marry up. The floorboards, from an old school gymnasium, continue up the side of the tub in place of panels. They are painted white, like the floor.

recycled *bathroom*

This bathroom belongs to salvage specialist Mark Rochester and his artist wife Talya Baldwin. In Mark's own words, everything in their home has come from somewhere else.

The sink, faucets (taps), toilet, bathtub, tiles, radiator, mirror, and floor are all salvaged. Older sanitary ware such as this is likely to have different fittings from pieces made today, but an experienced plumber should have no trouble with them. Mark recommends finding an older plumber who has worked with such fittings earlier in his career. Dealers in architectural salvage may be able to recommend suitable plumbers.

The Victorian claw-foot tub is appropriate for the age of the cottage. Before installing an antique tub yourself, consider its weight, not only for possible transportation costs but also to see whether the floor (usually upstairs) can take it—particularly when the tub is filled with water and a person! Another thing to consider is that it may need re-enameling. Going for the lowest quote may be a false economy, and always check what is covered by a guarantee. Some cheaper re-enameling treatments may make the tub difficult to clean or use, and you may always have to run cold water before hot.

Opposite: The house had previously been "modernized" with a small uPVC double-glazed window but Mark replaced it with a salvaged Victorian sash window, making the opening larger to accommodate it. The radiator once helped to heat a Victorian candle factory, while the 1930s Royal Doulton toilet and cistern were reclaimed from a hospital.

Above right: The basin and brass faucets also came from a hospital. Forming the backsplash is a line of seventeenth-century Delft tiles.

COLD

Opposite: Some of the basic, white, chain-store tiles have been cut down and interspersed among uncut squares, creating an original, tailor-made look. The narrow frieze of tiles near the top spells out the children's names in the dots and dashes of Morse code, although "no one's ever noticed," admits Posy. The coat hooks were discovered in a dumpster (skip). Kitchen and bathroom upcycling designer Nick Kenny created the vanity unit supporting the basin, fashioning its door from a zinc washboard and the handle from a brass lock.

Right: Nick Kenny also supplied the "odd couple" taps—both recycled—along with their vintage "hot" and "cold" signs. The mirror came from a Paris fleamarket, while the basin was bought on eBay.

hacks *plus vintage*

This bathroom, belonging to garden renovation expert Posy Gentles, is a mix of chain-store basics with vintage finds unearthed from dumpsters (skips) and rummage sales. It's a small room, carved out of a rear extension, with no window, only a roof light. Posy decided to reposition the tub to run across the width of the room, rather than along it, and to build a three-quarter-height wall up one side so that the end of the tub could host a shower area. The basin sits on the other side of that wall, cleverly maximizing the usable space.

Posy kept the decorative treatments simple. The white ceramic wall tiles were the cheapest and most basic she could find, but by cutting some into different sizes, she has achieved an original and tailor-made look. The bathtub, too, is a standard design from a chain-store bathroom supplier, but the recycled zinc panels on the side, which originally covered a rooftop in Paris, make it unique. They are also a more practical solution than tiling because they can easily be removed if there is ever a plumbing problem.

chapter five

halls and stairs

The first impression others will have of your home will come from the front door and then the hall. It is here you stamp your character and state whether you prefer historic authenticity or are a modernist at heart. Halls and stairways often offer wonderful decorating opportunities, with more wall space for bigger pictures, but front doors, halls, and stairs are also where the original architecture of your home will have the greatest impact. Inappropriate replica or replacement doors, windows, and stairs can blight a property. Fortunately, there are still lots of original fittings out there just waiting to be upcycled—often very inexpensively.

Left: Thomasina paints pictures for movies and sometimes she is allowed to keep them. This example, which she painted "in a Correggio style," appeared in the film *Hotel Splendide.* The stained and frosted glass helps to stop it fading in the sunlight.

Opposite: Thomasina's vivid green hall and stairway complement the "Indian-Caribbean," mid-century modern palette present in the rest of the house: she has lovely bright greens, reds, and yellows on her kitchen units, and on cushions and sofas. Using such an eye-popping color on the wall of the hall turns the space into a "highlight." In the rest of the house, the wall colors are pale and neutral.

decoration *and display*

Halls and stairwells offer some of the best decorating opportunities in the home, with plenty of wall space to display collections. Photographs, pictures, and mementoes will always be noticed by anyone entering or leaving the house. A collection of mirrors, picked up cheaply at garage sales and junk shops and hung together, will make a narrow hall seem much wider and brighter. And if there are lots of them, it doesn't matter so much what the individual mirrors look like. As these are spaces you only pass through en route to somewhere else, they're also appropriate for making a big statement with glorious wallpaper or a giant painting.

Look out for narrow secondhand furniture—you can always paint it if you don't like the color—or hack chain-store furniture with a coat of paint. But don't forget that the hall and stairs link the rooms of your house together, so think about what the colors and patterns will look like when all the doors are open.

Upcycling can also mean using your predecessor's decorative schemes. When you move into a new home, you don't have to set about changing everything. Look at what you can reuse or live with comfortably. You can always make major changes at a later date, although you may find that your upcycling and hacking philosophy means you no longer have to.

The hall opposite makes a dramatic statement with the beautiful Chinese-style wallpaper covering one entire wall. It had been put up by the previous owners of this house, now owned by writer and pop-up caterer Helen Frame and her partner Lee Shale. When you move into a house, always consider how to reuse your predecessors' decoration. If it's still in good condition, you may as well save your pennies until it needs redoing. Halls are a spectacular place for introducing pattern in an otherwise neutral background, and one wall of outstanding wallpaper won't break the bank.

Mirrors make narrow spaces seem wider and throw more light into dark passageways. You can find mirrors of all kinds—usually very cheaply—in any junk shop or rummage sale. Strip, paint, or gild them, or hang them together in collections.

Opposite: Helen Frame fell in love with this beautiful Chinese-style wallpaper years before she looked at the house with a view to buy. When she saw it on the wall of the hall, she was "thunderstruck—it felt as if it was meant to be." The little mirror was bought in London's Portobello Road for the downstairs bathroom of her previous home, the table at a local secondhand store.

Right: Easy to pick up and move, traditional hat and coat stands are useful storage, provided that your hall is the right shape. Find them in secondhand stores or on the internet.

Safety is a key issue on stairs, and a worn carpet can be more of a slip hazard than bare wood, especially if it is loose or torn. If you can't afford to replace it or want to try something new, rip it out and have fun with some DIY, until you have the budget to buy what you really want. However, you may decide to stay with your temporary creation.

Before painting a staircase, clean and sand the wood down thoroughly. Mark out any stripes or pattern with masking tape, coat with a primer, followed by two coats of your chosen color of floor paint. Many people like to have contrasting risers and treads, or contrasting banisters and spindles, or a "runner" up the stairs—the choice is yours.

If you think, though, that decorating a staircase is limited to a choice of either carpet or paint, then welcome to the world of staircase upcycling. Tiles, mirrors, wallpaper, or varnish can all update a tired staircase—and none of it is expensive.

Above left: The stairs were a recent addition to a loft conversion and their "new pine" look didn't fit with Posy Gentles' Victorian house. The solution was to fix inexpensive mosaic mirror tiles—more usually a feature of bathrooms—to the stair risers, adding light to a dark stairway, and paint the treads in a heritage brown color.

Above right: Joanne McQuinn hadn't intended her decorators to strip her stairs and hall back to pine, so she painted this yellow "rug" on the stair landing to make the pine effect less obvious.

Opposite: Tim Braden's house is a modern conversion from a community center, and the stairs have clean, airy lines, allowing light into the stairwell. Open stairs like these generally never need any more done to them than just sanding and varnishing.

lighting

Upcycling and hacking have transformed the world of lighting over the past few years. Industrial lights from factories, stores, train stations, and even parking lots are being recycled. People are wiring up all sorts of objects, such as cans, jars, and bottles, to turn into lamps, experimenting with different colors and designs of electrical wire. If you love trawling rummage sales and thrift stores, you'll find vintage lampshades that will transform a chain-store lamp base into something completely original.

It's time to look at "old-fashioned" lighting again—the little lamp that belonged to your grandmother, which has been sitting at the back of a cupboard for longer than you can remember, might be just the right eclectic note to add individuality to a modern interior.

new *traditionalists*

Replacing the ubiquitous cream card lampshade with one made of lace, frills, ruffles, or velvet—or gluing or stitching such traditional trims to a shade yourself—will introduce charm and character to any room.

In the 1950s and '60s, there was much less lighting choice to be found in stores, so it was common for housewives to make their own lampshades, using the fabric of their choice and sewing it onto a frame. Then they added a fringe, bobbles, or other trim. Today, you can search for lampshade-making kits on the internet, along with video tutorials, books, and instructions. Alternatively, use offcuts of fine fabrics or silk scarves, which always seem to turn up at thrift stores and rummage sales, to make unique lampshades.

There are stores that specialize in vintage lighting but, if you can afford to be patient, you will probably find your ideal light at a considerably lower price on the internet or in thrift stores or estate sale shops (house clearance sales). If you buy "silk" shades (fabric shades are usually called silk, even if they are made of something else), then you can usually wash them gently in warm water to spruce them up—at your own risk, of course! If they are made of card, a gentle wipe-down will be sufficient.

If you buy a secondhand light or turn something into a lamp, is it safe? In most countries you don't have to be a qualified electrician to wire or rewire a lamp, but you do have to know what you're doing. It's not just about the risk of electrocuting yourself —faulty household wiring is a major cause of house fires. You can buy fittings to pop into lamps, but if you have any doubt about your competency or about the wiring of something you've bought, consult a qualified electrician.

Previous page: A painted and distressed standard lampstand upcycled by Goldfinger Factory designer Rasha El-Sady with a shade made from lace bedspreads by Fein & Cooper.

Opposite: This modern fabric shade bought from a gift store is the perfect partner for an old French, glass and bronze wall light found at a fleamarket. When choosing a shade, think about how its color will affect the light cast: darker shades will focus light above and below the shade, while paler ones will create a more diffuse light.

Above left: Joanne McQuinn bought this stunning chandelier from Belgium via eBay. Chandeliers vary hugely in price, and top-quality ones are always expensive, but there are definitely bargains to be had if you look hard enough.

Above right: A champagne bottle converted into a light, with a shade made from a lace bedspread by Fein & Cooper. Special adapters are available that fit into the neck of a bottle. The electrical wire trails down on the outside, so there's no need to drill holes into the glass.

industrial *chic*

Reusing or upcycling industrial lighting is becoming increasingly popular, and it is happening in three ways. First, lights from twentieth-century factories, stores, and other commercial premises are being recycled for domestic use. Second, lighting is being made from waste materials—anything from redundant pipework to old CDs—that would otherwise be thrown away. And third, the practical draftsman's lamp—Anglepoise is probably the best-known brand—has emerged from the study and the office to take its place in the living room, kitchen, and bedroom.

The ingenious examples of upcycled lighting featured on these two pages have all been made in the Goldfinger Factory, a charity near London's Portobello Road. This "upcycling hub" not only upcycles discarded items but also designs and creates new objects from waste material. The pieces are made and restored by disadvantaged Londoners, then sold to "trendsetters with a social conscience."

Today's softer-effect bulbs mean that upcycled lights like these don't necessarily need shades. The "Pipe Lights" (opposite), for example, would be ideal in a kitchen, where you need practical task lighting, but don't want to run cabling or drill holes in the ceiling.

Above, from left to right: A number of designers are involved with the Goldfinger Factory, creating something new out of waste material, not only from buildings that are being demolished or renovated, but also from materials discarded after temporary high-profile events, such as London Fashion Week. The shiny reflective surfaces of the CDs in the "CD Table Lamp," designed by Ben Rousseau, Goldfinger Factory's guest creative director, create atmospheric ambient lighting; the "Celebration Chandelier," made from champagne corks and high-power LEDs, was designed by Alkesh Parmar and would make a stunning center light in a living room or bedroom; these "Offcut Lights", made from leftover blocks of timber ply, provide good overhead lighting.
Opposite: These spiderlike "Pipe Lights" have been fashioned from the copper remnants of an old heating system from a house renovation,

Today's lighting knows no boundaries—lampshades can be made from anything from blancmange molds to buttons, and lights can be sourced from factories, boats, farms, and offices. If there are old-fashioned light fittings in a house when you move in, don't automatically discard them. Clean them up and rediscover their charm.

Clockwise, from top left: Helen Frame uses recycled blancmange molds as lampshades; Tim Braden spray-paints old metal factory lampshades; this unfashionable but charming glass shade came with Joanne McQuinn's house; a glass funnel from a school science laboratory upcycled into a pendant light shade; a lampshade made of card with a sheet music motif; Lucy Dickens bought this storm light at a repro lighting store; Posy Gentles' vintage exterior light fitting, found at a rummage sale, is perfect for coping with the steam in her kitchen; an old-fashioned game cover used as a shade; it took Posy hours to stitch all these buttons onto the plain shade of a wall light; Penny Rich's 1930s light came from a Ministry of Defence office; a vintage medical lamp from France; a French "Holophane" glass pendant shade from the 1920s—Holophane is a type of glass patented in the US in the 1890s, and the word is used today for all ribbed, frosted glass shades, offering maximum light with minimum glare.

chapter seven

gardens

The term "garden room" defines current attitudes to gardens—we furnish them and we decorate them. For those who hate to throw things away, gardens are a perfect place for upcycling. Garden furniture has migrated inside, while interior fittings can be planted up outside. The choice is no longer between cheap terracotta or plastic pots and expensive designer pottery. You can plant up anything from plumbers' piping and zinc trash cans to old fireplaces, sanitary ware, Wellington boots, and soda cans. If something cracks or wears out, fill it with plants.

don't throw *anything away*

Not so very long ago, all the containers featured on these pages would have ended up in landfill. Now an old dustpan, a hospital trash can, and several empty soda cans are sprouting pretty flowers and trailing foliage.

Many of the photographs here are of Posy Gentles' garden. Posy specializes in renovating gardens. She says that you can use almost anything as a container for plants, "provided that it's not too shallow—you need space for the roots." And, although many plant catalogs specify which plants are suitable for container gardening, Posy believes you can put virtually all plants in pots.

The main issue is drainage. If an old sink or bin is cracked and leaky, that makes it a perfect candidate for planting, and if you have metal or wooden containers, you can drill holes in them. However, it's difficult to do this with ceramic or stone. Posy's suggestion is to put a thick layer of gravel at the bottom of the container, which will offer some drainage. In the end, if a plant doesn't look happy, change the container. As she says, "Containers offer lots of opportunity for experimentation."

Above left: Garden designer Fern Alder has planted up an ancient iron dustpan, fixed to the wall, with sedums. She is the force behind Full Frontal, a local community initiative that encourages people to plant their front gardens creatively—with lots of recycling.

Above: A humble hospital trash can has been reinvented by Posy as a container and planted up with fuchsias from a local market.

Opposite: San Pellegrino drinks are a favorite with Posy's family. When empty, holes are drilled in the bottom of the colorful cans, to turn them into planters—here, for diascias.

Is there anything that can't be used as a planter? The answer is "No," judging by these pictures, although the container does need to have some depth to accommodate the plant roots, meaning that shallow dishes and bowls are less suitable. Drainage is important: a leaky jug, pitcher, bowl, or sink makes a perfect planter, so you don't have to throw away favorite pieces of china. Take them outside and plant them up.

bowls *and boots*

If there isn't enough drainage in your ceramic containers, you can drill holes, but use a ceramic drill and wear safety glasses. Then plant the containers up, using potting compost and a small amount of plant food. Gardeners have traditionally been advised to put broken crocks at the bottom of pots to improve the drainage. However, a recent study showed that broken crocks at the bottom of containers made no difference to growing a healthy plant.

There's a trend for upcycling old shoes and boots by planting them up. Wellington boots work well because they're waterproof, but often leak as they age. You could also use walking boots. Or even high-heeled shoes—but there's not much room for soil, so try plants that grow in cracks of stone, such as thyme or succulents.

Above left to right: An old ceramic sink hosts *erigeron* daisies; Fern Alder used to be a ceramicist and she fired ant drawings onto this salvaged "ants in your pants" toilet bowl; planting up can be as easy as dropping a small plant in a pot straight into a teapot; Fern has used a pair of worn-out Wellington boots for more daisies.

upcycled *plumbing*

Galvanized buckets, troughs, and planters are classics—available in every hardware store or chain DIY shop at very modest prices. Styles have barely changed over the centuries. When plumbing was in its infancy, every home would have had galvanized buckets, washing troughs, laundry tubs, and zinc free-standing baths. Now these humble, practical items make stylish planters. They are so simple and unfussy that they work in both traditional and contemporary interiors.

Vintage galvanized ware is still sold fairly inexpensively in thrift stores and at online auctions, but it's also worth looking around a modern plumbing store to see what you can turn into a planter. Pipework, for example, can be cut to length and up-ended, and you won't need much of it—you can pick up off-cuts very cheaply. You can also find useful containers to adapt to planters at florists' wholesalers and farm stores.

It's very easy to turn metal containers into planters. Punch or drill several holes in the bottom—between three and ten small holes for a five-gallon (approximately 20 liters) bucket is about right.

Opposite: Old zinc washing sinks and tubs ready for planting. These shapes and styles are still available at modern hardware stores.

Right: Fern Alder bought this planter at a rummage sale in France, because she was amused by it. It's been upcycled from vintage faucets, piping, and two small buckets.

Left: Containers add useful height to a garden. Choose different-sized pots and containers for a lovely layered effect, or even add pots to your borders to prevent the planting from looking "flat." These pots are on Fern Alder's terrace. On the far left is an old rusty fireplace from her previous home, which she often plants up with fiery-colored flowers. These are then reflected in the old mirror behind, brightening the space still further. The pots alongside are nestled in a length of piping used for laying drains and in a galvanized florists' bucket. The more conventional terracotta pots sit side by side with a pot of rose campions inside a toilet. Fern has fired drawings of ants onto the outside—a humorous decorative touch.

a place *to sit*

Garden furniture can be expensive—or it can be cheap white or dark green plastic, just like everybody else's. But there are lots of bargains out there, too, as long as you're prepared to put in a bit of work to restore or repair tables and chairs that have rusted or weathered, although sometimes all that's needed is a lick of paint. The internet is a rich source of secondhand garden furniture only a few years old, selling for a fraction of the original price.

It's not difficult to restore either metal or wooden tables and chairs (provided they are stable), although it does take a bit of time. Clean thoroughly with wire wool, sand them down, and use a primer before painting, then follow with outdoor paint for long-lasting results.

Above left: A vintage 1970s garden table with chairs in an unusual shape add character to this roof terrace. If you live in a modern house, built in, say, the 1960s or '70s, it's worth hunting down furniture styles from that era to create a look that complements the surroundings.

Above: Posy Gentles' teak garden bench, made comfortable and inviting with a chintz cushion, is a charming addition to the garden. The weathered look is always very attractive but make sure the seating is safe to sit on. If you need to restore teak or other hardwood outdoor furniture, don't use paint. Instead, protect them with a specialist outdoor varnish or stain them with a different color.

Opposite: Artist Lucy Dickens' garden seat is a bench nestled inside an old boat that has been cut in half and stood on end. Her husband, Tom, bought the boat cheaply from a ship chandlery.

upcycled *traditions*

Upcycling and hacking are about reusing waste materials, and in doing so giving your home personality and making the most of your budget. But they are also about craftsmanship and reworking old traditions for contemporary life. The photograph opposite features recycled tin lanterns from Morocco and an unusual bench made in Britain from coppiced logs.

If you walk through the souks in Morocco, you can see lanterns like these being made in the same way as they have been for hundreds of years. Similar traditions exist in the West, where craftsmanship is a key part of upcycling and has been for centuries. The bench, by furniture designer Rex Helston, is made of metal and thin ash poles, coppiced from a local wood.

Coppicing is an ancient tradition, where trees are cut down almost to ground level and then allowed to grow back. This regenerates them and allows for greater bio-diversity. Within a few years, the trees are cut down once again. For centuries, farm workers were allowed their own patch of hedgerow or woodland. In return for maintaining it, they kept the coppiced wood for firewood, thatching, walking sticks, and making "hedgerow" furniture, even their own coffins. Sadly, the practice of coppicing has declined, resulting in congested woods, a reduction in biodiversity, and wasted wood.

Opposite and right: Rex Helston's coppiced ash garden bench. He describes his furniture as "hedgerow furniture updated to a contemporary design." He uses ash, hazel, green oak, and other discarded woods that "would now probably just have been burnt on the edge of the field." By making such pieces of furniture, Rex is doing his bit to keep the centuries-old tradition of coppicing alive.

Above right: Beautiful garden lanterns from Morocco, made from recycled tin, would add character to any garden table. Throughout Africa and the Middle East recycled materials are widely used to create beautifully crafted items—look out for them when on vacation or in ethical, eco, or Fair Trade stores at home.

resources

Featured homeowners and artists

Fern Alder, garden designer
www.fullfrontal.org.uk

Talya Baldwin, artist:
www.talyabaldwin.com;
www.dunnockandteal.com (for
children's wall stickers)

Tim Braden, artist and sculptor:
www.timbraden.co.uk

Christopher Bucklow, artist:
www.chrisbucklow.com

Anthony Daley, artist: c/o
www.flowersgallery.com

Lucy Dickens, artist:
www.lucydickens.com

Helen Frame and Lee Shale, pop-up
caterers: www.claudthebutler.co.uk

Posy Gentles, garden renovation
specialist: www.posygentles.co.uk

Penny Rich, writer and journalist:
www.pennyrichthewriter.com

Mark Rochester, salvage and renovation
of vintage furniture and industrial
antiques: www.rochesters.uk.com

Thomasina Smith, artist:
www.thomasinasmith.com

Useful websites

Online auction and private sale sites
www.ebay.com: the world's largest online
auction site

www.etsy.com: handmade, vintage,
reclaimed, and upcycled items from
individuals around the world

www.gumtree.com: classified
advertisement site for private buyers
(U.K. only)

www.preloved.com: online auction site
for secondhand items

Movie and theater set recycling

www.dresd.co.uk: sustainable clearance
of movie and TV production sets for
resale

filmbizrecycling.org: U.S. site for
reuse, recycling, upcycling, and
reclaiming of movie and theater sets
for a range of uses

www.set-exchange.co.uk: U.K. site
promoting free exchange and reuse
of theater props and stage sets

Kitchens and bathrooms

www.emeryetcie.com: Emery et Cie tiles

www.nickkenny.net: upcycled kitchen
and bathrooms from vintage and
salvaged furniture by Nick Kenny

Markets

To find good markets with recycled,
upcycled, or handmade items, do an
internet search for "vintage markets"—
the words "upcycled" and "recycled" still
produce very mixed results. A search for
"best markets for handmade goods" is
useful in providing addresses for online
sites, but less helpful in finding local
markets.

Lighting

www.feinandcooper.com: lampshades
made from antique lace or tablecloths;
they also sell lace panels

www.stiffkeylampshop.com: specializes
in restoration and retailing of period
lighting

www.urbancottageindustries.com:
make-your-own light kits, spare parts for
lighting, colored electrical wire, recycled
components for lights, etc.

Gardens

www.fullfrontal.org.uk: U.K. community
initiative to inspire people to plant up their
front gardens in innovative ways

www.rexhelston.co.uk: furniture design
made of sustainable British and coppiced
wood

www.themiddlesizedgarden.co.uk:
author Alexandra Campbell's blog about
gardening in less than an acre, with tips
for saving time, money, and effort,
including recycling and vintage

General upcycling, salvage, vintage, and antiques

www.antiquesbydesign.co.uk: uses a combination of antiques, reclaimed items, and old materials to create furniture and accessories for house and garden

www.cliothemuse.co.uk: upcycling and bespoke upcycling of "yesterday's treasures"

www.goldfingerfactory.com: upcycled salvaged lighting and furniture

www.theoldcinema.co.uk: London store dedicated to vintage, antique, and retro movie furniture and artifacts

www.re-foundobjects.com: recycled, upcycled, and designer ceramics and homewares

www.salvo.com or www.salvo.co.uk: directory of dealers, and some replica and reproduction architectural salvage

www.trainspotters.co.uk: industrial lighting and salvage

Miscellaneous

www.jali.co.uk:fretwork panels and shutters, made to order

www.janconstantine.com: handmade embroidered and felt fabric designs for cushions and other homewares by Jan Constantine

www.peacheydovecotes.com: Gerry Peachey, maker of kitchen units, as well as shepherds' huts and dovecotes

www.scarletandviolet.com for flowers and vases

Transportation

If you're buying privately, there are a number of online delivery auction websites, such as www.shiply.com. These make transporting items much cheaper than it has been in the past. You register what you want transported, what size it is, and other details, then carriers bid for your business.

index

acknowledgments

A huge thank you to Simon Brown whose stunning photographs captured the spirit of all the lovely houses so brilliantly. And also to the team at Cico Books: Cindy Richards, Helen Ridge, Louise Leffler, Fahema Khanam, Sally Powell, and, most all, Gillian Haslam, who has masterminded it all brilliantly. Thank you to dear friends who let us photograph their homes and to all the lovely new people we met who welcomed us into their homes. They are Joanne McQuinn, Thomasina Smith, Posy Gentles, Minna Ford, Lucy Dickens, Tim Braden, Penny Rich, Mark Rochester, Talya Baldwin, Helen Frame, Lee Shale, Fern Alder, and The Goldfinger Factory, especially Oliver Waddington-Ball.